HOW TO PLAY
ELECTRONIC
KEYBOARDS

HOW TO PLAY ELECTRONIC KEYBOARDS

Mike Beecher and Rosalyn Asher

Elm Tree Books
International Music Publications

Copyright © 1984 by International Music Publications

First published in Great Britain 1984
by Elm Tree Books Ltd
Garden House, 57-59 Long Acre, London WC2E 9JZ

in association with

International Music Publications

2nd impression 1986

British Library Cataloguing in Publication Data

Beecher, Mike
  How to play the electronic keyboard.
  1. Electronic organ
  I. Title   II. Asher, Rosalyn
  786.7   MT192

  ISBN 0-241-10990-6
  ISBN 0-241-10991-4 Pbk

Printed in Great Britain by
St Edmundsbury Press Ltd, Bury St Edmunds, Suffolk

INTRODUCTION

The electronic keyboard, with its ability to create the tone colours of traditional instruments as well as the sounds of a synthesiser, can be one of the most versatile and exciting instruments to play. It is now available in many shapes and sizes, from small portables to large organs with two or three manuals plus pedals.

Despite their differences in sound and effects, to play any of these instruments it is necessary to have a good keyboard technique. We also believe that in order to offer you the greatest independence when learning and choosing new music, it is necessary to read and have a basic knowledge of music, although 'playing by ear' as an additional skill is by no means discouraged.

Apart from a large section that helps you to play the electronic keyboard, this book includes information on the history, development, parts and functions of the instrument together with hints on its purchase and maintenance.

The last section of the book includes ideas for extending and improving your playing as well as a reference of notes, chords, music and suggested registrations for the tutor section of the book.

Remember that whatever kind of instrument you have, the way to make the most progress is WITH YOUR EAR!

CONTENTS

INTRODUCTION

PART 1: ABOUT THE ELECTRONIC ORGAN

PART 2: PLAYING THE ELECTRONIC KEYBOARD

PART 3: IDEAS FOR THE FUTURE

SUPPLEMENT FOR NOTE DIRECTORY AT END OF TEXT:

PART 1 ABOUT THE ELECTRONIC ORGAN
A BRIEF HISTORY AND DEVELOPMENT OF THE ELECTRONIC KEYBOARD

The electronic keyboard has become an immensely popular instrument. Basically, the range may be described as a group of instruments which generate and process sounds electronically. The sound source consists of electrical circuits which generate oscillating electrical currents. These are then amplified into sound waves through the medium of a loudspeaker.

The history of the electronic keyboard stems from the earliest portable pipe organs, takes in the great church organs, mighty theatre instruments, the invention of Hammond's tone wheel and drawbars and brings us to the present generation of all-electronic organs.

With the development of the synthesiser in the 1960's, the soundmaking possibilities of keyboard instruments were greatly expanded and by the late 1970's, there was a proliferation of both synthesiser and organ keyboards. However, it was with the development of the mini-keyboard in 1981 that the 'electronic keyboard revolution' may be said to have begun.

Early electronic keyboards.

The recent and rapid development in electronic technology has produced considerable changes in the design of electronic keyboards. The American inventor, Laurens Hammond, led the way to the all-electronic organ with his 'tonewheel' sound-producing system in 1934. The spinning tonewheels, each about the size of a large coin, were turned by an electric motor at a constant speed. The different number of teeth on each wheel produced electrically a different note as they revolved in front of a magnet, with each note being activated from the organ keys and pedal board by interconnecting electrical wires and gears.

TONE WHEEL

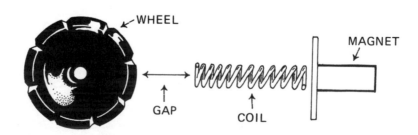

ABOUT THE ELECTRONIC KEYBOARD

Hammond's organ also had nine sound pitches for each key on the manual, connected to nine drawbars or 'tone bars'. Each drawbar could then adjust the individual volume levels of its pitch. The pitches were related to the notes of a church-organ rank of flue pipes, with the 16' set of tonewheels representing 16 feet long open pipes, sounding lowest notes and the 8', 4', 2' and 1' sounding the same notes at the next highest pitch each time.

FOOTAGES

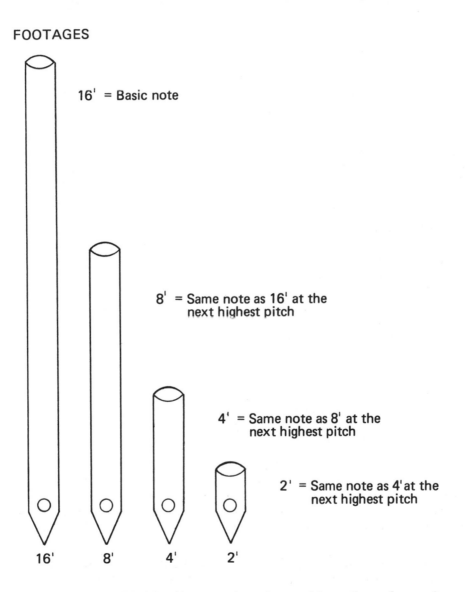

16' = Basic note

8' = Same note as 16' at the next highest pitch

4' = Same note as 8' at the next highest pitch

2' = Same note as 4' at the next highest pitch

16'   8'   4'   2'

Other drawbars were also added by Hammond to give a wider variety of tones by means of 'mutations' — pitches at different intervals to those created by the above:— 5⅓', 2⅔', 1⅗', 1⅓'.

By adjusting the drawbars many different sound combinations could be produced.

From Spinet to portable keyboards.

The first Spinet organ appeared in 1949. These early instruments had a 44-note manual with a 12-note pedal board, and created sound waves from the electrical oscillations of valves. Later on, the bulky valve circuits were replaced by smaller and more reliable transistors.

At the heart of a transistor organ was the circuitry that generated the top twelve notes on the keyboard. These notes, or frequencies, were then successively divided by two to obtain all the lower notes. Therefore, notes on an electronic instrument do not go out of tune with one another like those on a piano but can all be adjusted by one 'tune' control to match other instruments.

The raw oscillator frequencies are selected by the manual or pedal keys and sent to filters and other sound processors that simulate electronically the brass, woodwind, string and other instrument tones. There are still transistors inside most contemporary keyboards although much of the circuitry has now been replaced by IC's (integrated circuits) that can hold many hundreds of transistors on silicon 'chips'. The final sound is amplified and played through loudspeaker units. The largest 'furniture' keyboards have free-standing speaker cabinets with self-contained amplifiers for stereo effects. As many as 8 full-range speakers can be incorporated including the 'Leslie' type that rotates the sound (either mechanically or electronically). Much of the processing of sounds is now done by a microcomputer inside the keyboard which scans the controls and switches continuously, noting any changes made.

The keyboard revolution.

The application of the latest technology to keyboards has virtually made them into micro-computers in their own right.

Now we have the 'Digital Band' and the 'Micro Orchestra' that can create the most authentic sounds at the touch of a button. Many gimmicks have also become essential facilities for the budding keyboard player and even the most inexperienced should be able to play complete pieces on the electronic keyboard in a very short time.

The easy-play aids have introduced a second generation of features which expand music-making activities even further. Special music or keyboard notes have LED (Light Emitting Diode) indication of what to do next and you can learn a piece as quickly or slowly as you like, being prompted along the way. A built-in music printer transcribes composed pieces into traditional notation, and bar codes, magnetic strips and RAM/ROM cartridges have become as accepted a means of storing music as the analogue or digital cassette recorder.

Keyboards can memorise not only a single sequence, but can also hold every element of your composition, from the kind of rhythm to be used to the full accompaniment, melodies and counter melodies. Now that the keyboard has also taken on the function of a multitrack tape recorder, it is possible to record a piece into a keyboard all at once or take each part step by step. Some instruments can be linked together to play from one keyboard or a home computer.

As well as remembering the notes, complete registrations for the whole instrument can be dialled from a voice setting computer. Even the process of making sounds on the electronic keyboard is changing. Analogue sounds have become digital sounds — either by additive or subtractive synthesis. Completely new principles of soundmaking are used in FM tone generation but the results are more realistic, and better related to traditional acoustic instruments than ever before. Pulse Code Modulation (PCM), by using digital PCM recordings stored in complex LSI (Large Scale Integrated Circuit) chips, has enabled accurate reproduction of the sounds of real percussion instruments.

The arrival of low cost multi-sound sampling keyboards will ensure continued development. So anything can be reproduced from a dog bark to a chord played by an entire symphony orchestra, and a link to a microcomputer enables you to analyse every part of the sound on a TV screen. The potential of the contemporary electronic keyboard is no longer limited to the sounds within the instrument, but may be expanded by the exploration of any live sound that can be captured.

The point has now been reached when it is quite difficult to say how a particular instrument works, for there are many special circuit designs used by manufacturers which are closely guarded secrets. Even the small portable single keyboard may offer many of the facilities provided by the largest and most expensive instruments, since the microcomputer based technology used by both can provide a complete orchestral sound from easy-play features to a full percussion accompanist, as well as the facility for music reading and printing.

THE MAIN TYPES OF ELECTRONIC KEYBOARDS.

Although there are now a wide variety of keyboards available, these may be grouped into four basic types:

1. Small portable battery or mains powered single mini-keyboards:

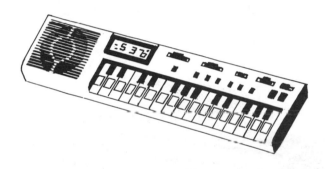

2. Larger portable battery or mains, single or dual standard sized keyboards:

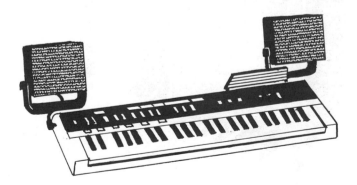

These lightweight instruments are very popular and although small, still manage to retain many features of the larger instruments, including built in amp/speakers, easy play features, preset sounds, auto rhythms, the ability to record or transpose melodies and a split keyboard for the accompaniment section. Although some of the smaller ones have a range of available sounds, they are not designed to play more than one or two of these simultaneously.

This is why many players use a 'multitrack recorder' to combine sounds. As an additional feature, some of the larger portables include free-standing pedal boards.

3. The free standing Spinet comprising of (a) the single manual type
                                       (b) the dual manual type
                              and (c) types (a) or (b) with an additional synthesised keyboard.

These are the most compact types of 'furniture' instruments for home and have enjoyed considerable popularity in recent years. Besides offering facilities found on types 1 and 2, they have a larger range of preset sounds and the ability to combine different sonorities. They generally have two 44-note manuals and a 13-note pedal board. This is one of the main advantages of this type of keyboard as it enables the player to choose from a vast selection of available organ music of many different styles. In addition, the swell pedal enables the player to constantly control and vary the volume of the music.

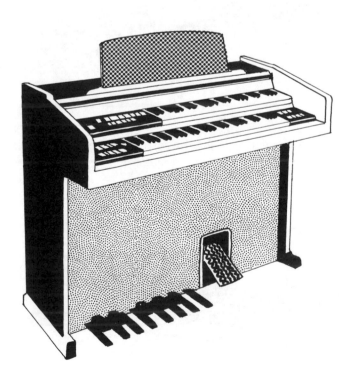

4. The Console Organ: These are the grand home organs that offer the widest choice of sound suitable for a variety of styles of music from popular to serious. It looks like a theatre organ with its shaped 'console' and roll top of polished wood. On these instruments, there is sometimes a third manual used for solos or to create special sounds. The pedal board can have an increased range of 17, 25, 30, or 32 notes. The larger keyboards and pedal boards are descendants of the 'classical' organ. However, whereas on the Spinet and some console pedal boards it is only possible to play one note at a time (monophonic), on the classical and other console pedal boards it is possible to play more than one note at a time (polyphonic).

ELECTRIC PIANOS

In addition some single keyboard instruments specialise in traditional keyboard sounds, such as Piano and Harpsichord.

These instruments do not come with a foot operated volume control, but have a sustain pedal instead. The amount of sustain can be varied by the use of the rotary control on the facia, as can the overall volume by the use of the rotary volume control. A certain amount of light and shade can also be achieved by playing the keyboard with more attack, either for whole chords or to bring out a melody.

It is best to buy the instrument with the largest range of notes that you can afford. This is usually six octaves and will allow you to play most keyboard music.

Some instruments have the tabs Piano 1, Piano 2, and usually Harpsichord 1 and 2. The first tabs operate traditional sounds, whilst the others are for the mellow electronic keyboard sounds used by groups today.

It must be said that initially, these are not the easiest of instruments to play.

Using piano technique on an electronic keyboard requires the player to be very accurate and disciplined, as the keyboard has a very light touch. However, once this is achieved, a range of keyboard sounds are available from the harpsichord of early keyboard music to the Electric Piano of modern popular music which can be used through a group's sound system.

A Chorus Tab is also sometimes included. This is an organ sound, and should be played and used accordingly.

THE MAIN ELEMENTS AND FUNCTIONS OF AN ELECTRONIC KEYBOARD

Learning to play an electronic keyboard does not just mean playing the notes correctly, for all but a few instruments have facilities that enable you to become a 'one-man band'. As you become more experienced, you will be able to go from one keyboard to another and quickly spot the main sections of the new instrument and the functions available. At one time, the most sophisticated features were only found on the largest and most expensive keyboards. Now with the development of microcomputer technology, an increasing range of low cost instruments have innovative features housed in compact single manual portables.

This section identifies the main functions you are likely to find on a modern keyboard instrument.

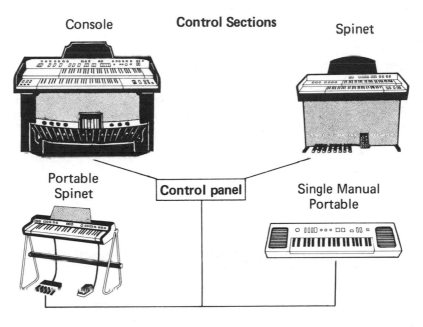

Control Sections

Console

Spinet

Portable Spinet

Control panel

Single Manual Portable

Looking At Control Sections.

Every control panel of an electronic keyboard is provided with pushbuttons, touch pads, plastic rocker tabs, or levers that SWITCH something directly on or off. Very often, a built-in coloured LED (Light Emitting Diode) will show the 'on' position. Other controls make continuously variable adjustment by means of rotary knobs, click or smooth sliders or levers, pushwheels, pedal or up/down touch pads.

A well designed instrument will be laid out so that the available functions are in labelled sections. Sometimes this is simply done by colour-coded buttons, or an LCD (Liquid Crystal Display) or LED alphanumeric (showing letters and numbers) display indicating chosen sounds, and even keyboard chords or notes played in a recorded sequence. Beginners can select a keyboard that has LEDs to show which manual or pedal notes or chords to play next, while sophisticated models may have illuminated buttons to indicate the settings at a glance.

If the instrument is a larger-sized console organ with upper and lower manuals (and possibly a third solo manual) plus pedals, look for the functions relating to each of these. There will be separate sound sections for each manual and pedals, as well as sections that provide special effects. The diagram below shows the 4 main soundmaking sections: SOLO, ACCOMPANIMENT, RHYTHM and EFFECTS.

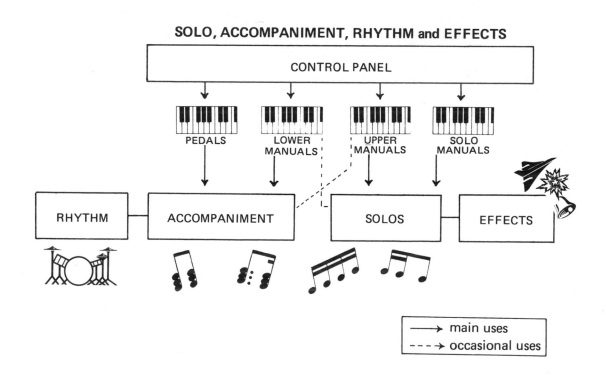

SOLO, ACCOMPANIMENT, RHYTHM and EFFECTS

Easy Play Features.

The SOLO or melody part is usually played by the right hand on the upper manual (spinet or console) or right hand part of the keyboard (single keyboard). Some keyboards have features that produce a professional sounding solo right from the start. These generally enable you to play one finger right hand melodies while the 'auto' function provides an accompaniment. These and other 'easy play' features are intended to help you to get started. They can supply you with an automatic accompaniment that can often be controlled simply with one or two fingers of the left hand. Even instruments with pedal boards often have a full accompaniment that provides an automatic bass line until you are able to play this on the pedals yourself.

The auto accompaniment can consist of BASS line, SINGLE FINGERED or FINGERED CHORDS (groups of notes to accompany a melody), ARPEGGIO (notes of the chord played one at a time) and drum rhythm unit. A MEMORY button remembers the last left hand chord played, so that you can release the notes until a new chord is required. KEY PLAY or TOUCH START brings in the whole accompaniment only when you play a left hand note or chord.

Several instruments are able to remember the chords, melodies and other settings that you require for one or more pieces or sequences of music. These are stored either in the circuitry of the instrument or transferred to a cassette recorder as digital information (a series of high speed pitched pulses). Although the names of 'auto' functions vary according to the manufacturer, every instrument includes a detailed explanation of these aids in its instruction manual.

The Solo Section.

The sounds provided on a keyboard for right hand melodies can either be MONOPHONIC (playing one note at a time) or POLYPHONIC (playing several notes at once). They are selected by means of PRESET switches or sliding DRAWBARS. These will again vary considerably from instrument to instrument.

Some of the most common types of monophonic sounds or voices are:
a) String types e.g. Solo Violin.
b) Brass types e.g. Trumpet.
c) Woodwind types e.g. Flute or Clarinet.
d) Percussion types e.g. Guitar.
e) Classical types e.g. Diapason or Harpsichord.
f) Synthesiser type e.g. Wah Wah or Synthe Chopper.

Polyphonic voices include:
   Full Harmony, Orchestra Ensemble, Singing Voice (ah, uh) and Big Band,
with specials such as:—
   Vocal Ensemble (4 voice choir), OPS (Own Programme Storage) and Touch Sensitive Piano.

Drawbars

Drawbars or Harmonic Tonebars are sliders that add sounds as they are pulled out. The flute-like pitches that are produced may be combined at different volumes to give many different sounds. The main drawbar pitches (or footages) are 16′, 8′, $5\frac{1}{3}'$, 4′, $2\frac{2}{3}'$, 2′, $1\frac{3}{5}'$, $1\frac{1}{3}'$, and 1′. (In exceptional cases $1\frac{1}{7}'$, $\frac{8}{9}'$, $\frac{4}{5}'$, $\frac{2}{3}'$, are added).

Drawbar settings are often shown on keyboard music by a row of 9 numbers – they correspond to the main drawbars from the lowest, 16′ pitch to the highest, 1′ pitch in the order given above. For example, 80 7003 051. The nine figures are plit into three groups partly to make the registration easier to read and more importantly to show deep tone (2 numbers), basic tone (4 numbers) and drawbars for brightening the sound (3 numbers).

Each drawbar is given a value (0 to 8) which corresponds to most keyboard drawbar labelling (often felt as a 'click' setting when moving the drawbar), although a few instruments are numbered 0 to 10 and some guesswork is needed to match values. Drawbars may also be colour-coded to make choosing of individual footages easier.

On two-manual keyboards with drawbars, the lower manual usually has 7 footages: 8′, 4′, $2\frac{2}{3}'$, 2′, $1\frac{3}{5}'$, $1\frac{1}{3}'$, and 1′.

The selection of sounds for a particular piece of music is called the REGISTRATION (Reg.) In Part 2 of this book, 'Playing the Electronic Keyboard', there will be a suggested Registration for each piece of music. In Part 3 of the book there is a separate section called 'Hints on Registration'.

Percussion Drawbars.

Many organ-style instruments, especially those with drawbars, also have Percussion drawbars (or switches). They do not make drum sounds, as you might imagine, but produce a short 'percussive' sound when a new key is played. Several pitches can be available as with the standard drawbars. Usually the short time taken for a percussion sound to die away can also be adjusted – from a brief 'ping' to a longer piano-type decay.

The most used percussion footages are: $5\frac{1}{3}'$, 4′, $2\frac{2}{3}'$, 2′, and $1\frac{3}{5}'$. Other percussive sounds that can be switched on or off are CLICK – adding a mechanical click like the early tonewheel organs, PICK – for banjo and mandolin realism (with or without REPEAT for strumming at various speeds), and CHIFF – for organ pipe or flute 'puff' at the start of a note.

As contemporary technology enables very realistic percussive sounds to be reproduced – such as piano, guitar, harp and vibraphone – traditional instrumental sounds (along with new ones like Cosmic) are being increasingly used.

The Accompaniment Section.

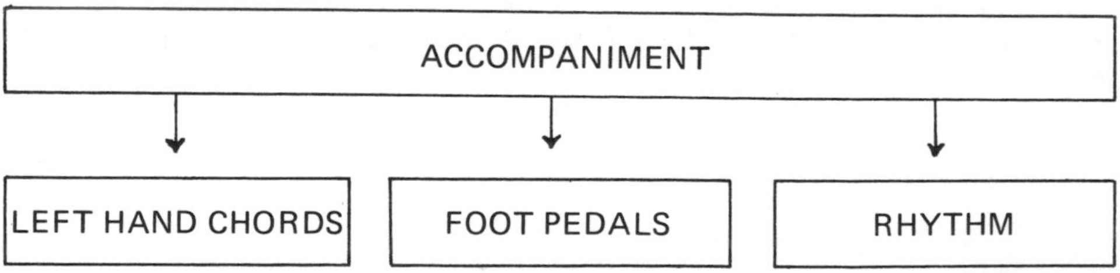

Left hand chords.

Single manual instruments will either use a preset sound over the whole keyboard or will have a 'split' keyboard. The left hand usually provides the accompaniment from the lower (left) end of the keyboard so that the right hand solos can be played at a suitable volume level on the remaining keys. Instruments with two or three manuals will usually play the accompaniment on the lowest manual with the left hand. Although there will be less choice, the sounds available will be taken from the presets or drawbar voices already described for the solo section. If there is an 'Easy-Play' feature, then it is also likely that special accompaniment sounds will be provided — like piano, guitar, clarinets, and so on. Sophisticated instruments will even put complete ensembles at your fingertips — such as Big Band, Country & Western, Rock, and Dixie.

Pedals.

Once you have acquired a reasonable skill on manuals, footpedals can extend your musical accomplishments. The pedals usually provide the 'bass line' of an accompaniment, just like the double bass in an orchestra, the tuba in a band, and a bass guitar in a group.

Here are some typical voice presets for the pedals:
Double Bass, Tuba, Diapason, Bass Guitar, 'Cello.

Most of these sounds are deep footages at 16' or 8' and will match the pitch of the lowest notes on the keyboard.

Other aids.

Other useful controls found on some instruments are:

SUSTAIN — for lengthening the decay of a sound after a key has been released.
ACCENT — a percussive pitch at the start of a sound.
STACCATO — which makes each sound short and detached.
MEMORY — which holds on a sound indefinitely after its release, or until a new one is played and held similarly.

Rhythm.

Nearly all electronic keyboards have a percussion section. The fact that an instrument has its own built-in 'drummer' ensures that any rhythmic accompaniment (from 'Easy Play' features) is always synchronized with what you are playing. It will not be long before all electronic drum sounds will be digital 'samples' of the real thing. Here are some of the sounds that could be found on a good keyboard:—
Bass Drum, Snare Drum, Hi-Hat (open, closed), Tom-tom (low, high), Bongo (low, high), Cymbal (crash).

Some of these drum sounds will be playable from buttons or manually-operated touch pads, but the drum rhythm will be run automatically for the length of a piece. Some of the most common rhythms to be found on electronic keyboards are:—
Rock, Swing, Bossa Nova, Rumba, Calypso, Boogie, Waltz, Cha Cha, Tango, Samba, Soul, Disco and March.

Balancing manuals and pedals.

Most electronic keyboards have a VOLUME slider or rotary control for each sound group, that operates independently from any others. Occasionally, one section, such as the accompaniment, may not have a level control and may only be adjusted in volume by setting the instrument's rhythm and solo sections to it. However, individual control of each section is preferable and will enable you to 'balance' the sounds together easily. On some keyboards, especially organs, you may find a balance control that sets Upper and Lower manuals gradually louder and softer and vice versa. When playing pop music, the rhythm section and the bass line are usually louder than the accompaniment and the melody, even though listeners may not realise it because they are concentrating on the melody. In dance band music and pieces that have become 'standards' over the years, the rhythm is generated by the music itself, so that a loud drum beat is unnecessary, but the melody will need to be more prominent.

Volume setting.

Turning up the volume too high on one or more sections of an electronic keyboard can sometimes cause distortion of the sound. This is often done deliberately by rock musicians but is generally undesirable. In fact most keyboards usually sound better when the volume is not at maximum. Most experienced players will set the Master Volume control first so that the final volume of the whole instrument is below 75% to give plenty of 'headroom' as sounds are layered together.

On the other hand, the volume swell pedal (optional for portable keyboards), is usually set fully on (pushed forward and down), except for introductions, changes of mood or tempo, and endings.

External amplifier.

When using an external speaker or complete amplifier and speaker system, the same care has to be taken. Many instruments have a LINE OUT socket which provides a suitable signal sound source for connection to an amplifier. When the amplifier is part of a hi-fi system, it is likely that a MICROPHONE input will be too sensitive and will overload and cause distortion at all settings of your hi-fi amp volume control. Instead, use inputs marked PRE-AMP AUX (Auxiliary), LINE, or TAPE to connect a keyboard. Ready-made leads with plugs at both ends are available from most electronic, D.I.Y. or hi-fi shops.

Some keyboard instruments will not cut out their built-in loudspeakers when you connect the SIGNAL (or LINE) OUT to an amplifier or tape recorder. This is generally quite useful except during recording, when monitoring of the sound entering a tape recorder or cassette machine only will be required. An easy way to turn off the built-in speaker is to plug in a pair of headphones, if a headphone socket is provided.

BUYING AN ELECTRONIC KEYBOARD

Buying an electronic keyboard is certainly not an easy task as there are many manufacturers, each with their own range of instruments. Try to visit several music shops so that you can *hear* and compare as many different instruments as possible. Even if you do not play, you can learn a great deal about the electronic keyboards available by talking to dealers, reading manufacturers' brochures and current keyboard magazines which regularly report on new models with their specifications. Above all, try to go to a keyboard specialist where there will probably be a salesperson who will be able to demonstrate some instruments and take you through their features step by step.

If you cannot afford a new keyboard you could either buy one through a special purchase scheme or try to find a secondhand instrument. Always ask an experienced keyboard player to inspect a secondhand instrument as you may find that something you thought to be a bargain could prove extremely expensive in repairs! Also, check that spare parts are still available for an older instrument. For this reason it is not advisable to purchase an instrument made by a company which no longer exists.

Take your time to decide so that you purchase the best instrument you are able to afford. The one with the most knobs, buttons and lights is not always the best buy. An instrument with a reasonable number of quality sounds, an 'Easy Play' system and reverberation or (on small portables) sustain, is adequate for a beginner. Remember, it is always the *sound* and not the gimmicks that produces a keyboard of lasting quality.

LOOKING AFTER YOUR KEYBOARD

Dust and dirt are the main causes of faulty operation. To protect your instrument always cover it when not in use.

Never stand on a pedal board, and always treat mechanical controls, foot controls such as the swell pedal and any built-in switches with care.

Like any electronic instrument, physical damage to components inside can occur if the keyboard is handled roughly, especially if portable instruments are dropped or knocked.

Avoid placing liquids on the keyboard. If these get inside the instrument it could easily cause damage.

Cleaning.

You can clean all the black and white *keys* by wiping them with a soft, slightly dampened cloth; when dry, polish lightly with a soft dry cloth. More stubborn marks can usually be removed by a scratch-free polish, but *never* use spray directly on the keys.

Carefully clean the *control panels* with a soft cloth. Move any sliders right up and then right down during cleaning and avoid dropping dirt into the slots. When dry, wipe over lightly with a clean dry cloth. Never use 'thinner' type liquids, or sprays, as they may cause discoloration or stains. Some panels may be of a special material that require extra care. Refer to your instruction manual if this is so.

The free-standing Spinet or Console will be encased in solid wood, wood veneer, or simulated wood plastic. Clean all *wood surfaces* with a wax furniture polish, unless the organ manufacturer recommends otherwise. It is worth noting that a polish containing silicone will leave a permanent coating which cannot be removed if the organ cabinet needs refurbishing.

All *plastic surfaces* can be wiped clean with a damp cloth, then lightly polished with a soft dry cloth.

SETTING UP AND MAINTENANCE OF THE INSTRUMENT

Setting up your keyboard.

Most keyboards will be completely self-contained and unless powered by battery will simply require to be plugged into a mains source. The manufacturers' instruction book should take you step by step through the setting-up procedure, including the selection of a basic sound for you to start playing.

Always check that the mains cable has a suitable plug correctly wired up and fuse-protected for inserting into the nearest mains socket in your home. Avoid long lengths of cable if possible and check that the operating voltage is correct.

If your instrument is a portable one, it may have a small internal amplifier/speaker system built-in, while still offering an alternative output socket. You can connect this via a suitable lead to your hi-fi system (Aux input, or similar) to a separate Combo amplifier, or to a mixer or tape recorder for recording your music.

Most keyboards have a headphone socket to enable you to use your own mono or stereo headphones (low impedance type) to practise privately. Large instruments will have their own separate speaker cabinets that link directly to the main console. Smaller portables often have optional pedal control via rear connection sockets and you should check these requirements with your supplier. If the instrument is battery operated then make sure the correct batteries are inserted according to the instruction manual.

Some instruments have a voltage selector at the back. The manufacturer's handbook will warn you of this. Make sure that it is set to match your local supply. Also, these instruments will usually have a welded two-pin plug of the continental type. A suitable adaptor to the British three-pin plug can be obtained from your local electrical shop. However, as these pins are of the same size, it is not possible to discern which is Live or Negative. If when you have plugged in you are aware of a hum or a rushing background sound, switch off the instrument and the socket and reverse the adaptor. When you switch on again, the noise should have disappeared. Mark the adaptor and plug accordingly so that you will always plug in the right way round. Switch off the instrument when not in use, and always switch on the socket before you switch on the instrument.

Check whether a music stand is supplied with the instrument. Many small portable instruments can of course be played on a table with the music close by, or on a separate stand.

When positioning the instrument, always note any advice given in the instruction manual.

What to do if there is a fault.

If the instrument does not appear to be functioning correctly in any way, then immediately switch it off and consult your instruction manual. If this does not provide a remedy, then contact your supplier. In general, unless an instrument is secondhand and quite old, it should operate quietly, with just a discernible hiss from the speakers. Any loud electronic hums or gurgling may be the sign of a faulty instrument and should be checked by a qualified electrician. One last but very important point — never tamper with the inside of an instrument, unless you are qualified to do so. There is a wide range of voltages involved that can cause an electric shock, and possible damage to microcomputer components may be caused by their wrongful removal.

PART 2 PLAYING THE ELECTRONIC KEYBOARD

As there are now a large number of electronic keyboard manufacturers each with their own specific directions and special effects, the bulk of this next section of the book is devoted to the development of a basic keyboard facility. This is introduced with the aid of rudimentary musical notation. However, suggestions for how to use the more common features found on some electronic keyboards, such as the 'auto chord' and basic registration, will also be indicated before each piece of music.

SUGGESTED REGISTRATIONS

Registrations or voice settings given in this book are intended as a guide.

On keyboards containing drawbars the settings represent 0–8 switch positions.

If the UPPER MANUAL registration was given as 88 8888 888, it would mean that all the drawbars – 16', 5 ', 8', 4', 2 ', 2', 1 ', 1 ' and 2', would be at their fullest setting.

For the LOWER MANUAL, –– 8888 888 represents a full setting of the 8', 4', 2 ', 2', 1 ', 1 ' and 1' drawbars.

The PEDALS only indicate a setting for the 16' and 8' plus a 'percussive' drawbar.

If your instrument only has a limited number of drawbars, select the given settings for these as a basic introduction to suitable sounds. In the absence of a 'guitar' voice on your keyboard, try experimenting with another 'percussive' voice.

Most important of all – experiment for yourself and try to create a balanced sound between the melody and accompaniment.

SITTING POSITION

Position your stool so that it is facing the middle of the keyboard.

Dual Manual Electronic Organ   Single Keyboard

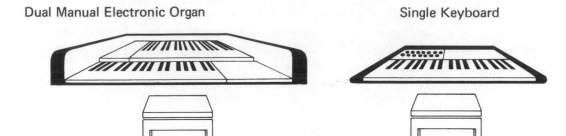

An organ stool is available from your local dealer. Although a little more expensive, the adjustable ones are preferable.

When playing the organ, you do not have your feet on the ground for support, so try and achieve a position on the stool where you can reach the pedals comfortably, and have the stool near enough to the keyboards so that you do not have to lean on the upper manual.

If you have a dual manual electronic keyboard, sit so that with elbows bent you can place your *right hand* over the notes of the UPPER MANUAL and your *left hand* over the notes of the LOWER MANUAL as shown in the diagram below. If you have a single keyboard, place your hands over the keys so that your *left hand* is able to operate the section devoted to the chord functions.

Always play the notes with the pads of your fingertips. Your wrists should be level with the tops of your hands and forearms. Unlike a piano, an electronic keyboard does not require a striking action to produce a sound, for each key is simply an 'electronic switch' that activates a circuit. Only on a few special instruments will you find that the *way* you play alters the volume of the sound or attack.

If your instrument includes a pedal keyboard, the *ball of your left foot* should be able to reach these keys without difficulty.

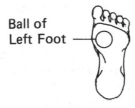

Ball of
Left Foot

Your *right foot* is used to control the SWELL PEDAL which regulates the volume of sound.

Swell Pedal

Always try to maintain a relaxed but correct posture at the keyboard.

THE KEYBOARD

Musical *sounds* known as NOTES are represented by the first seven letters of the alphabet:
A B C D E F G

The keyboard is arranged to form a regular repeated pattern of *seven white and five black notes.* The black notes are grouped into alternating sets of two and three.

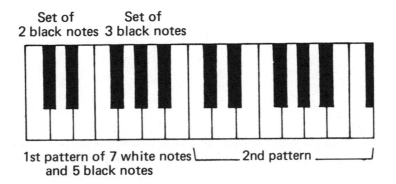

Set of
2 black notes

Set of
3 black notes

1st pattern of 7 white notes⌐_____ 2nd pattern _____⌐
and 5 black notes

25

Although the notes of the pedal keyboard may have a different shape and colour, they share the same pattern. Here are diagrams of the manual and pedal keyboards with the white notes labelled.

Manual Keyboard

Pedal Keyboard

C D E F G A B C D E F G A B C

C D E F G A B C

└── An Octave ──┘

Notice that the *same* letter name occurs on every *eighth* consecutive note played on the keyboard. This distance is called an OCTAVE.

The note C may always be found to the left of a set of two black notes. With the index finger of your *right hand,* find and play every C on the upper manual. (If you have a single keyboard, when the upper manual is indicated in this book, use the right hand side of your instrument and when the lower manual is indicated, use the chord functioning left hand side).

Now with the index finger of your *left hand,* find and play every C on the lower manual. If you have an instrument with a pedal keyboard, with your *left foot,* find C.

Finally, with the aid of the diagrams above, try to find and play the following notes:
F   E   B   D   G   A

FINGERING

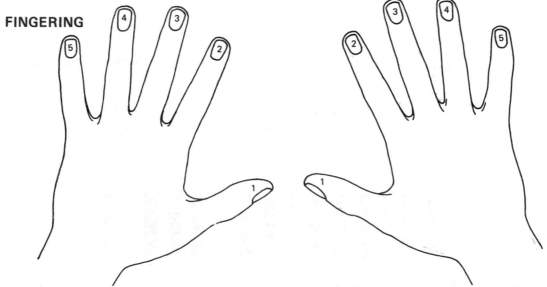

The numbers 1 to 5 are used to help you to know which fingers are used on certain notes.
1 — Thumbs; 2 — Index fingers; 3 — Middle fingers; 4 — Ring fingers; and 5 — Little fingers.

With your *right hand thumb* on any upper manual C EXCEPT the top one play the following:

Right Hand Fingering: 1   2   3   4   5

Exercise 1:

```
                              G
                    F         5         F
              E     4                    4     E
        D     3                                3     D
  C     2                                            2     C
  1                                                        1
```

Now try Exercise 1 starting on a different C.

Using the lower manual, with your *left hand thumb* on any C, play the following:

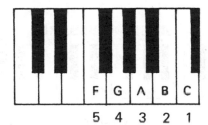

Exercise 2:

Left Hand Fingering: 5   4   3   2   1

```
  C                                              C
  1     B                                  B     1
        2     A                      A     2
              3     G          G      3
                    4     F    4
                          5
```

Remember when you depress the keys that you will not alter the volume by the way you play the notes (unless you have a touch sensitive keyboard). This is set with your right foot on the *swell pedal* or the *master volume control* on the main panel. Therefore, always play the notes lightly and smoothly. You should release one note as you play the next to ensure that sounds are joined (legato). This is an important aspect when learning to play an electronic keyboard.

PLACING MIDDLE C

Use the 8' pitch tabs on lower and upper manuals. On the electronic keyboard the note middle C is the lowest C to be found on the upper manual and the C directly beneath this note on the lower manual:

Middle C (UPPER MANUAL)

↑ Middle C (LOWER MANUAL)

On a single keyboard with four octaves, middle C will be the third C from the bottom.

SINGLE KEYBOARD

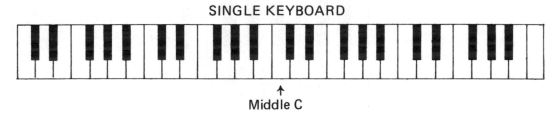

↑
Middle C

On smaller or larger keyboards, middle C is usually to be found nearest the centre of the instrument.

Now, with your right hand thumb on the upper manual middle C and your left hand thumb on the lower manual middle C, try playing Exercise 3. (This is Ex. 1 and Ex. 2 combined.)

Exercise 3.

						G				
				F			F			
			E					E		
		D							D	
Middle	C									C
R.H. and L.H. Fingering	1	2	3	4	5	4	3	2	1
Middle	C									C
		B							B	
			A					A		
				G			G			
					F					

If you have a pedal keyboard, play Exercise 3 again — this time adding the bottom C with your left foot. Hold this note down all through the exercise.

RHYTHM Notes of Different Lengths —

Most music has a regular pulse — a steady beat like the ticking of a clock or the beating of a heart. With these examples in mind, clap a steady beat.

The musical symbol for a note which lasts for ONE BEAT is called a CROTCHET or QUARTER NOTE. It looks like this  or ⌐ . Clap a row of crotchets at a steady speed:

♩ ♩ ♩ ♩ ♩ ♩ ♩ ♩

The musical symbol for a note which lasts for TWO BEATS is called a MINIM or HALF NOTE. It looks like this ♩ or ⌐ and lasts *twice as long* as a crotchet. Clap a row of minims holding each one for TWO beats:

♩   ♩   ♩   ♩
1 2 1 2 1 2 1 2

The musical symbol for a note which lasts for FOUR BEATS is called a SEMIBREVE or a WHOLE NOTE. It looks like this **o** and lasts *twice as long* as a minim. Clap a row of semibreves holding each one for FOUR beats:

o   **o**
1 2 3 4 1 2 3 4

NOTE VALUES

1   2   3   4

♩ ♩ ♩ ♩   crotchets (quarter notes) worth ONE beat each

♩   ♩   minims   (half notes   ) worth TWO beats each

o   semibreves (whole note) worth FOUR beats each

Clap the following rhythm:

Exercise 4:

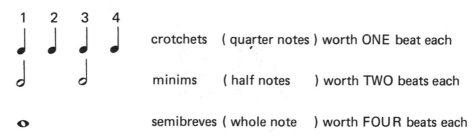

To make the reading and counting of music easier and to give it rhythmic direction, groups of notes are divided into small sections called BARS containing a specified number of beats. Bars are divided by vertical lines called BAR LINES. If we divide Exercise 4 so that there are 4 beats in every bar it will look like this:

Exercise 5:

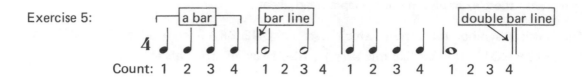

Count: 1   2   3   4   1   2   3   4   1   2   3   4   1   2   3   4

A DOUBLE BAR LINE indicates the end of a main section of music or the end of the music. With your right hand thumb on middle C (upper manual), try playing the first PHRASE (musical sentence) of 'Au Claire de la Lune'. The rhythm is the same as the one used in Exercise 5.

AU CLAIRE DE LA LUNE

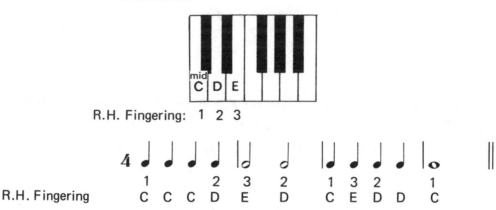

With your left hand thumb on the D above middle C (lower manual), try the middle section of the song:

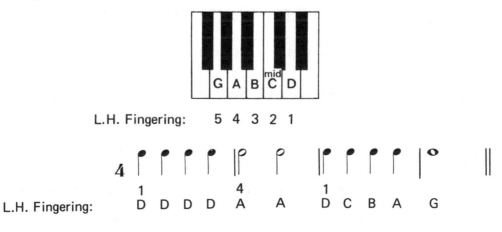

Now try the whole tune:

AU CLAIRE DE LA LUNE

┌─────────────────────────┐
│ ‖: :‖   Repeat the music
│   Between these signs
└─────────────────────────┘

R.H. Fingering   1   2   3   1   3
                C   C   C   D   E   D   C   E   D   D   C

L.H. Fingering: 1   4   1
                D   D   D   D   A   A   D   C   B   A   G

R.H. Fingering: 1   2   3   1   3
                C   C   C   D   E   D   C   F   D   D   C

TIME SIGNATURES

The sign to show how many beats there are in a bar is written at the beginning of the music. It is called a TIME SIGNATURE. It consists of two numbers written one on top of the

other e.g. $\frac{4}{4}$

So far we have only used the *top number* which indicates *how many* beats there are in a bar. The *bottom number* indicates what *kind of beat* is to be used. If the bottom number is 4, the beat is a crotchet (quarter note).

$\frac{4}{4}$ There are 4 crotchet (quarter note) beats in a bar

$\frac{2}{4}$ There are 2 crotchet (quarter note) beats in a bar

$\frac{3}{4}$ There are 3 crotchet (quarter note) beats in a bar

Here are some rhythms in each of the above times. Practise clapping them first — then using your keyboard, make up a tune to go with each one.

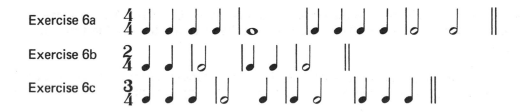

Exercise 6a $\frac{4}{4}$

Exercise 6b $\frac{2}{4}$

Exercise 6c $\frac{3}{4}$

PITCH

To indicate how high or low a note is to be played, it is placed on a musical ladder of lines and spaces called a STAVE. A stave has 5 lines and 4 spaces.

A STAVE

FIFTH LINE → ———————————————— ←FOURTH SPACE
FOURTH LINE → ———————————————— ←THIRD SPACE
THIRD LINE → ———————————————— ←SECOND SPACE
SECOND LINE → ———————————————— ←FIRST SPACE
FIRST LINE → ————————————————

NOTES ASCENDING   NOTES DESCENDING

THE TREBLE OR G CLEF

To fix the pitch of the higher notes a *Treble or G clef* is used. It is called a G clef as its symbol curls round the line on which G above middle C is written:

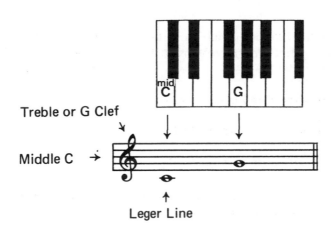

Treble or G Clef

Middle C →

Leger Line

When there is not enough room on the stave, extra lines called LEGER LINES are introduced to accommodate the notes. In the treble clef, middle C is written on the first leger line *below* the stave.

Find and play middle C and the G above on the upper manual. Within the confines of this book, the treble clef will always refer to the notes of the upper manual played by the right hand.

After you have clapped the rhythm through, try to play the following tune using notes G A and B

(Recommended registrations will always be included in the top left hand corner and rhythms in the top right hand corner.)

(To help you to use the suggested registrations indicated throughout this book, re-read the section entitled 'SUGGESTED REGISTRATIONS. on page 23.)

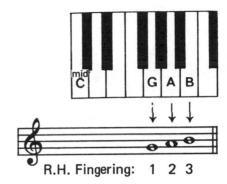

R.H. Fingering: 1 2 3

SIR CHRISTEMAS
(German Folk Tune)

Registration: Oboe 8' (00 4763 000)   Rhythm: March

NEW SYMBOLS: ♩. A dotted minim or dotted half note which lasts for THREE beats.

𝄽 A crotchet or quarter note rest which means *silence* for ONE beat.

NEW NOTES: C and D

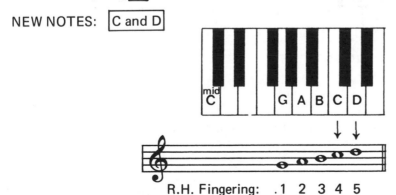

R.H. Fingering: .1 2 3 4 5

Always work out the rhythm before trying to play a new piece.

MERRILY WE ROLL ALONG

Registration: Flutes 8', 4', 2' (00 8605 000)   Rhythm: Swing

*The letter names marked with an asterisk over each bar (e.g. G *) may provide you with any of the following 'Easy Play' facilities: —

(i)   Play the melody with the 'auto chord' function in operation.

(ii) At the beginning of each bar, play the letter name that is written above the stave, on the *lower manual* with the 'auto arpeggio' facility in operation. Use the 8' stop.

OR (iii) Play the letter name written above the stave on the pedal board. To set up the pedals use the 8' stop and 'sustain'. The *'sustain'* control will make it easier to join the sounds together.

LOWER MANUAL G and D   PEDAL BOARD G and D

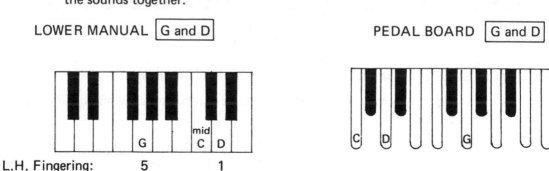

The STEMS of notes change direction on the middle line of the stave:

34

NOTES: | middle C D E and F |

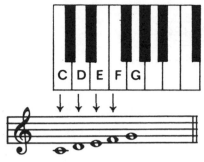

R.H. Fingering: 1 2 3 4 5

3/4 time. Clap the new rhythm first.

Remember, this sign ‖: :‖ means repeat the music.

Exercise 7:

Count: → 1 2 3 1 2 3 1 2 3 1 2 3 1 2 3 1 2 3 1 2 3

FRENCH FOLK SONG

Registration: Clarinet (00 7373 000)   Rhythm: Waltz

Lilting

LOWER MANUAL | C and G | PEDAL BOARD | C and G |

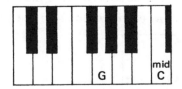

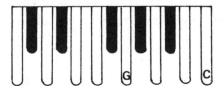

SHARPS

NOTE: | F SHARP (F♯) |

Make sure that your third finger
is over F sharp

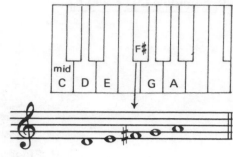

R.H. Fingering: 1 2 3 4 5

DRINK TO ME ONLY

Registration: Strings (34 3576 421)

Rhythm: Waltz

Quite slow

A sharp sign (♯) lasts until the end of the bar
unless it is cancelled by a natural sign (♮)

A tie = joins the value of the notes it binds
therefore 𝅗𝅥. (+) ♩ = 4 beats.

LOWER MANUAL

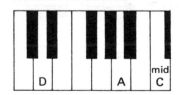

PEDAL BOARD

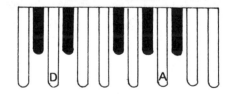

A SHARP (♯) raises a note to the nearest key on the keyboard. This distance is called a
SEMITONE. The arrows on the following diagram show each *semitone* on the keyboard.

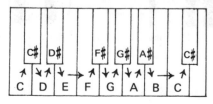

Find and play the following notes on the keyboard:— F♯ C♯ G♯ D♯ and A♯

THE BASS OR F CLEF 𝄢:

To fix the pitch of lower notes a *Bass or F Clef* is used. It is called the F clef as the dots of the symbol used are placed on either side of the line on which the note F below middle C is written. In the bass clef, middle C may always be found on the *first* leger line *above* the stave.

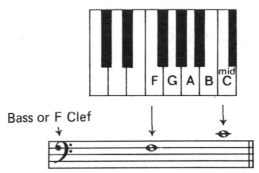

Bass or F Clef

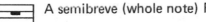

Within the confines of this book the bass clef will always refer to the notes of the lower manual and the pedal keyboard which are played by the left hand and left foot respectively.

NEW SYMBOL: A semibreve (whole note) REST which means *silence* for 4 beats.

This rest is also used for a full bar's silence whatever the time signature.

With your *left hand* on the *lower manual,* try the following exercise:

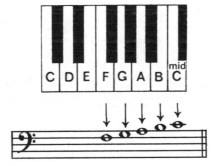

L.H. Fingering: 5 4 3 2 1

Exercise 8:

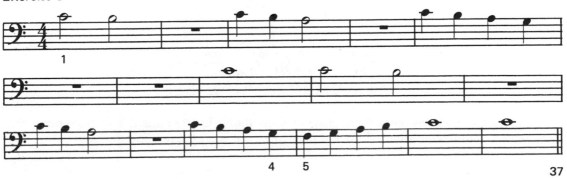

Now, using the *upper manual* try adding the right hand part to the tune you have just played in Exercise 8. Notice that when played separately, the right hand part often imitates the left hand part but moves in the opposite direction (Contrary Motion). When the hands play together they also move in contrary motion.

REFLECTIONS (Rosalyn Asher)

Registration: UPPER: Flute 8' (00 8000 000)   Rhythm: Nil
LOWER: Flute 8' (—— 8000 000)

A BRACE, shows that the two parts should be played together.

FLATS

A FLAT (♭) lowers a note to the nearest key on the keyboard — a semitone. The arrows on the following diagram of a keyboard shows each semitone.

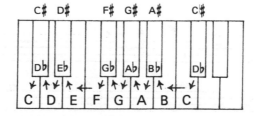

The names of the notes outside the diagram show that it is often possible to have more than one name for the same sound. Find and play these notes on the keyboard:

Bb   Eb   Ab   Db   and Gb

NOTE: B FLAT (Bb)

Make sure your fourth finger
is over the Bb

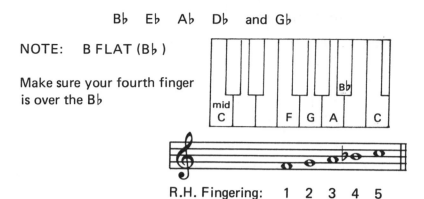

R.H. Fingering: 1   2   3   4   5

Thoroughly practise the right and left hand parts separately before trying them together.

GO TELL AUNT NANCY
(American Folk Song)

Registration: UPPER: Clarinet 8' (00 7373 430)   Rhythm: Swing
                LOWER: Flute 8' (—— 8403 000)

Quite lively

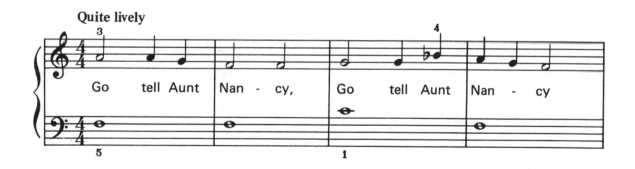

Go   tell Aunt   Nan - cy,   Go   tell   Aunt   Nan - cy

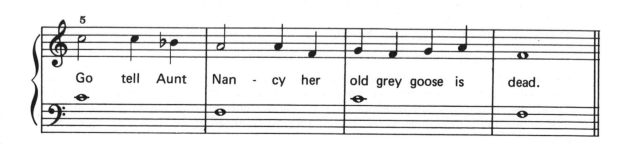

Go   tell   Aunt   Nan - cy her   old grey goose is   dead.

IRISH LULLABY

Registration: UPPER: Flute 4' (00 2800 000) Rhythm: Waltz
LOWER: Flute 8' (—— 8803 000)
Strings 8'

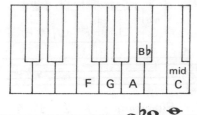

L.H. Fingering: 1 2 3 4 5

Lilting

Play F and C at the same time.

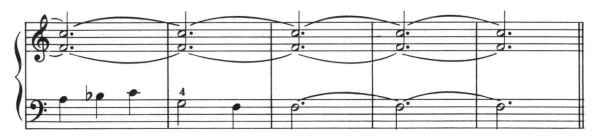

THE PEDALS

If your keyboard does not have pedals your left hand may play the pedal part when it is within the compass of your hand. If you have a standard spinet, the pedal board will consist of one octave of notes. Larger pedal boards, like manual keyboards, simply extend the note range.

To operate each pedal, lightly tap each note with the ball of your left foot. Always play from the ankle, without moving your knee up and down. As it is only possible to play one note at a time, it is important to aim accurately. Before you begin, examine the layout and the feel of the pedal board. However, try not to be tempted to look at your feet when playing.

The kind of shoe you wear is important — the best footwear is flat and flexible with a thin sole (e.g. slippers) to allow some physical contact with the pedals.

Fig. 1a Pedal notes are either (a) written on an extra bass stave e.g.:

Upper Manual

Lower Manual

Pedal Board

etc.

or   (b) added to the bottom of the bass clef stave e.g.:

Fig. 1b

Upper Manual

Lower Manual

Pedal Board

Notes to be played on the lower manual will have ascending stems and those to be played on the pedal board will have descending stems.

In this book method (b) is used.

Before trying the following exercises for left hand (lower manual) and pedal board, feel your position on the pedal board by finding the gap between Eb and Gb, and also feeling the groups of 2 and 3 black notes.

Try these exercises for left hand (lower manual) and pedal board.

Start by practising the pedal part on its own. Don't add the lower manual part until you are able to play from C to G on the pedal board without looking.

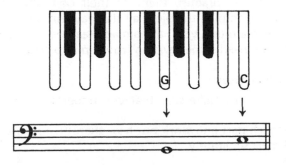

Ex. 9a
Lower
Manual
Pedal
Board

Rhythm: Disco

Ex. 9b

Rhythm: Waltz

NEW SYMBOL:  A minim (half note) REST which means silence for two beats.

Rhythm: Swing

Ex. 9c

HINTS ON PRACTICE

(a) General Hints:

Now that you have discovered the main elements necessary to play the electronic keyboard, to help you to learn pieces of music thoroughly and efficiently, it is important to organise your practise carefully.

(i)   Always choose a part of the day when you are relaxed.
(ii)   If you cannot have a room to yourself, use headphones (via the head phone socket) to practise privately.
(iii)   The amount of time varies according to personal concentration and work load, but you will make far better progress with shorter amounts of *daily* practise than with playing for several hours once or twice a week.
(iv)   Start by warming your fingers up with any appropriate exercises at the keyboard.
(v)   Organise your practise so that you work at a piece or pieces of music that are new or have not yet been perfected. Always do this at a *slow speed* and isolate the passages that you find difficult and practise them on their own. Only when these have been perfected should you try to play the piece all the way through.
(v)   Finally, play some of the music you have already learned (REPERTOIRE). Remember however that these may need some revision from time to time!

(b)   Learning a New Piece of Music:
(i)   Look through the music to make sure that you understand all the signs and symbols used.
(ii)   Clap the rhythm of each part and work out how these fit together.
(iii)   Play and learn each part separately.

(iv) Play the parts in pairs before putting them all together e.g.:
upper and lower manual parts together; upper manual and pedal parts together; and then lower and pedal parts together.

(v) When you are ready, play the piece through a *section at a time* with all the parts together SLOWLY and CAREFULLY.

(vi) When you have mastered any difficult passages, play the piece through from beginning to end. Always do this at a slow speed as it is then possible to control and *hear* what you are playing. Work the piece up to speed gradually.

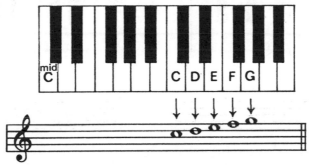

R.H. Fingering: 1 2 3 4 5

ODE TO JOY (From Beethoven's 9th Symphony)

Registration: UPPER: Oboe (Reed) 8'   (00 4675 432)   Rhythm: March
               LOWER: Flute   8', 4' (—— 4342 321)
               PEDAL: 8'   (4—(2))

Don't forget to try each part separately then put them together in pairs before finally playing it all through.

Allegro (An Italian term meaning 'lively').

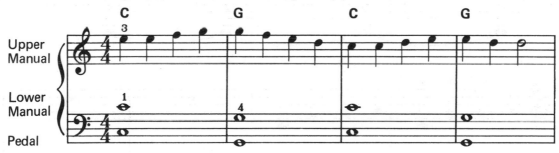

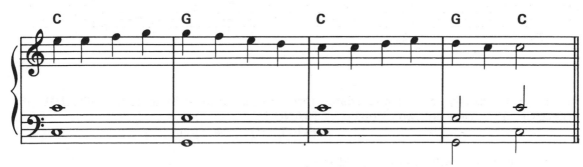

Italian terms are often used to indicate the TEMPO or speed of a piece of music.

FRERE JACQUES

Registration: UPPER: Trumpet   8'   (00 6888 543)   Rhythm: March
               LOWER: Reed 8'. Flute 8', 4' (—— 7788 422)
               PEDAL: 8'   (4—(2))

Practise playing from both Cs to G on the pedal board without looking.

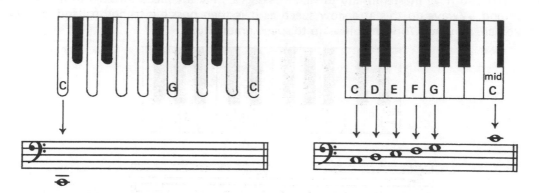

Moderato (An Italian term meaning at a moderate pace).

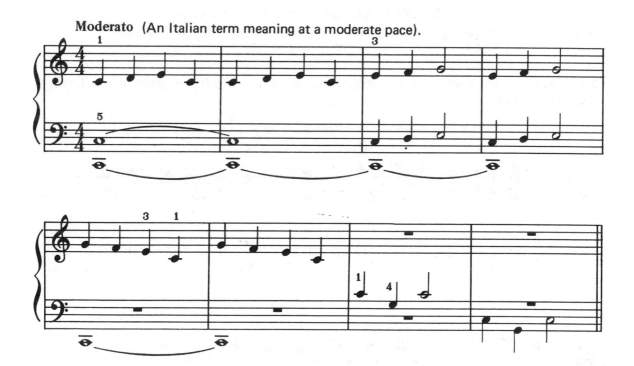

Italian terms, usually in their abbreviated form are also used to indicate the VOLUME of a piece of music. Here are two of them: PIANO (p) — soft
                                                                          FORTE (f) — loud

Try to control these with the SWELL PEDAL.

JINGLE BELLS

Registration: UPPER: Harpsichord or String (00 8888 866)   Rhythm: Jazz Rock
LOWER: Flute   8′, 4′   (—— 8600 000)
PEDAL: 16′ & 8′

CHORDS

Chords are a group of notes played simultaneously, usually to provide an accompaniment to a piece of music (HARMONY). The simplest form of a chord is a TRIAD.

A TRIAD consists of *three notes* and may be built on any note.

To build a triad on the note C —

(i)   The foundation or ROOT of the triad would be the note C.

(ii)   Add the THIRD note above the root

3	E
2	~~D~~
1	C

(iii) Finally add the FIFTH note above the root

5	G
	~~F~~
3	E
	~~D~~
1	C

This is the triad or chord of C. Try to play it on the lower manual with the recommended fingering.

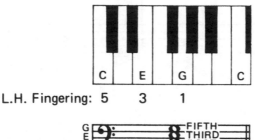

L.H. Fingering: 5   3   1

This chord does not have to be played with the root at the bottom (called the ROOT POSITION). It can be played so that the THIRD is at the bottom. This is called a FIRST INVERSION. Compare and play the root position and first inversion of the chord of C given below.

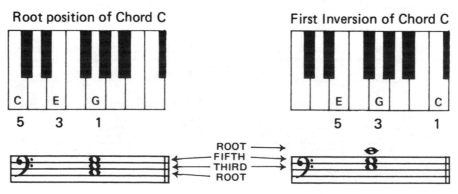

Notice that in the first inversion the *third* of the chord, the note E is now at the bottom, the *fifth* of the chord, the note G is above it, and the *root* of the chord, the note C has been moved up an octave so that it is now at the top of the chord. Memorise these two positions.

This chord can also be played so that the FIFTH is at the bottom. This is called a SECOND INVERSION. Compare and play the root position, first inversion and the second inversion of the chord of C given below:

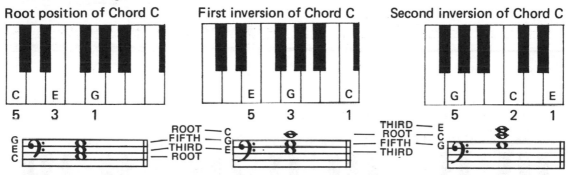

Root position of Chord C   First inversion of Chord C   Second inversion of Chord C

Notice that in the second inversion the *fifth* of the chord, the note G is now at the bottom, the *root* of the chord, the note C is above it, and the third of the chord, the note E has been moved up an octave so that it is now at the top of the chord.

CHORD BUILDING EXERCISES FOR THE LEFT HAND

Exercise 10a

Rhythm: Swing

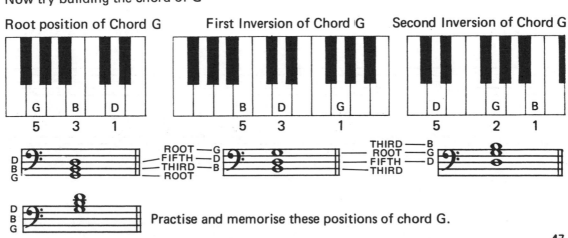

Now try building the chord of G

Root position of Chord G   First Inversion of Chord G   Second Inversion of Chord G

Practise and memorise these positions of chord G.

Exercise 10b   Rhythm: Waltz

Building the chord of F is achieved in the same way:

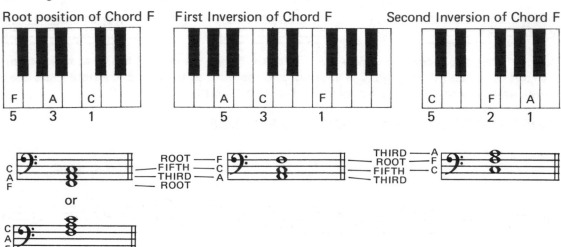

Root position of Chord F   First Inversion of Chord F   Second Inversion of Chord F

Practise and memorise these patterns and try the next Exercise.

Exercise 10c: Rhythm: Bossa Nova

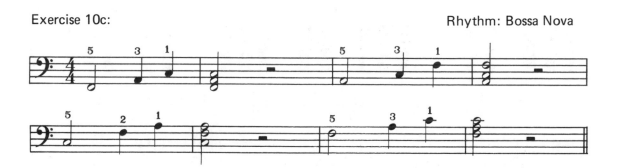

MIXING CHORDS

To accommodate the notes of the melody and to colour the sound produced, chords frequently change during a piece of music. Practise the simple chord changes in the following exercises. Many pieces of music use these chord progressions. Practise and try to commit them to memory. When you have mastered them try adding the root of each chord on the pedal board.

Exercise 11a:

Pedal → C   G   F   C
the root

Exercise 11b:

Pedal → C   F   G   C
the root

Exercise 11c:

Pedal → C   G   F   C
the root

Try a tune that we have played before but this time with left hand chords added to the accompaniment.

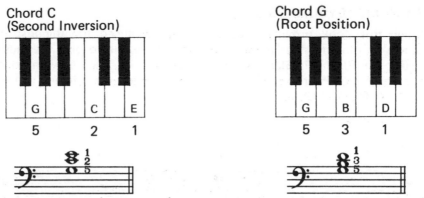

Chord C (Second Inversion)

Chord G (Root Position)

Practise changing between the two chords written above before trying the next piece of music.

NEW ITALIAN TERMS: MEZZO PIANO (mp)   — moderately soft
                           MEZZO FORTE (mf)   — moderately loud

ODE TO JOY

Registration: UPPER' Oboe (Reed) 8'   (00 4675 432)   Rhythm: March
            LOWER: Flute   8', 4' (—— 4342 321)
            PEDAL: 8'   (4—(2))

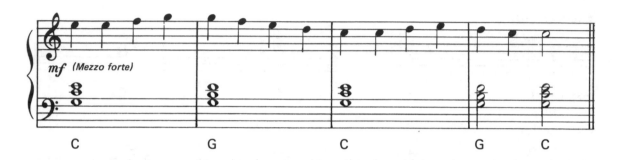

Pedal
the root: C   G   C   G

C   G   C   G   C

NEW SYMBOL: **C**   The time signature $\frac{4}{4}$ used to be called COMMON TIME. Sometimes
the sign **C** is written instead of $\frac{4}{4}$ at the beginning of the stave.

From now on, the bottom note of the bass clef will always be the pedal board part.

FOR SINGLE KEYBOARDS ONLY

Although this book provides music primarily arranged for the instrument with pedals,
the single or dual manual keyboard player will be able to play the music by initially concentrating on ROOT POSITION chords. To help you, each new chord is introduced in its
various positions. The root position chord may be decorated in any of the following ways:
(CHORD C: ROOT POSITION)

(i)   In $\frac{3}{4}$ time:

In examples (i) (a), (b) and (c), the rhythm is varied.
Example (i) (d) splits the notes so that they are played separately.
and example (i) (e) plays the root on the first beat followed by the two upper notes of the
chord on the second and third beats.

50

(ii) In $\frac{4}{4}$ time:

Examples (ii) (a), (b) and (c) vary the rhythm.
Example (ii) (d) plays the notes of the chord separately,
and example (ii) (e) plays the root on the first and third beats and the two upper notes of
the chord on the second and fourth beats.

When you have memorised these, try them out using chords G and F. These are not the
only possibilities. Try to make up some more. With practise, it will be possible for you to
incorporate the pedal and some of the lower manual notes with your left hand e.g. —

This could be played as this

or this . Alternatively, and more effectively you could bring the top

C down an octave, so that all three notes of the chord are within the compass of your

left hand.

NEW SIGNS: CRESCENDO (cresc)   —   gradually getting louder
                  DIMINUENDO (dim)   —   gradually getting softer
                  PIANISSIMO (pp)   —   very soft

I KNOW WHERE I'M GOIN'

Registration: UPPER: Flute 8', 4', 2' or Piano (00 8705 003) Rhythm: Waltz
LOWER Flute 8', 4' (—— 6402 000)
PEDAL: 8' medium, sustain (4—(2))

Slow and smooth

p I know where I'm go-in' And I know whose goin' with me;

Pedal board

I know who I love, But the Lord knows who I'll mar-ry!

pp Fea-ther beds are soft, And paint-ed rooms are bon-ny, But

I would leave them all For my hand-some, win-some John-ny.

52

NEW SIGN: FORTISSIMO (ff) — very loud.

GREEN GRAVEL

Registration: UPPER: Flute 16', 8', 4', 2²/₃' Clarinet (88 8874 322) Rhythm: Waltz
LOWER: Flute 8', 4'. Reed 8' (—— 8862 432)
PEDAL: 8' medium, sustain (6—(2))

Notice that this piece of music does not have a full bar at the beginning. It starts on the *third* beat of the bar. When this happens the missing beat or beats may be found at the end of the music. The last bar of this piece has the missing two beats.

FINGER EXTENTIONS

So far we have only used right hand melodies which cover five consecutive notes. Extending the range of your playing involves changing your fingering and extending the span of your hand during the music. In the next piece you will need to change your fingering on the *first beat of the sixth bar.* Always count the first bar with the complete number of beats as bar number one.

Practise the following chord changes (progressions) before playing the 'Caisson Song'.

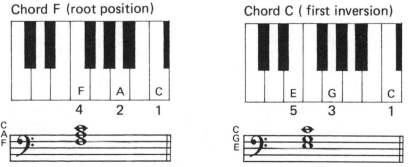

53

PEDAL NOTE F:

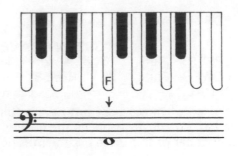

CAISSON SONG

Registration: UPPER: Reed 8' or Guitar (00 8856 322) Rhythm: March
LOWER: Flute 8', 4' (–– 6402 000)
PEDAL: 16' & 8' (5––(3))

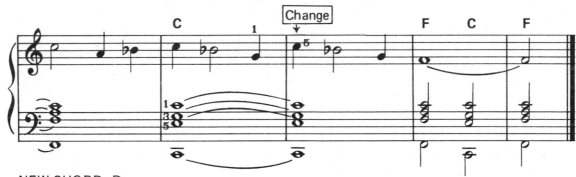

NEW CHORD: D

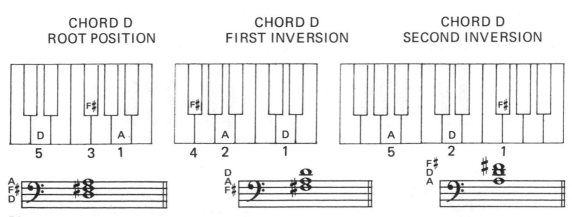

CHORD D ROOT POSITION	CHORD D FIRST INVERSION	CHORD D SECOND INVERSION

Practise the following chord changes before playing the next piece of music.

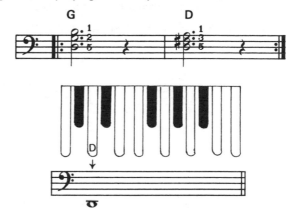

PEDAL NOTE D:

THE KEY SIGNATURE

LITTLE BIRD

Registration: UPPER: Oboe 8', Flute 16', 8', 4' or Pan Flute (88 8006 008)
LOWER: Diapason 8' or Piano   (—— 8853 000)
PEDAL: 8', medium, sustain.   (5—(3))   Rhythm: Swing

Notice that instead of writing the sharp sign in front of each F, it is written at the beginning of each stave and must be remembered all the way through the music. Sharps or flats written in this way are called a KEY SIGNATURE.

Practise the following finger extension exercises before trying the next piece of music. Avoid playing neighbouring notes when stretching from one note to another.

Exercise 12a:

R.H. Fingering: →1   3   4   5   3

Exercise 12b:

R.H. Fingering: →1   2   3   5   3

Play the following melody through a few times:

DOWN IN THE VALLEY

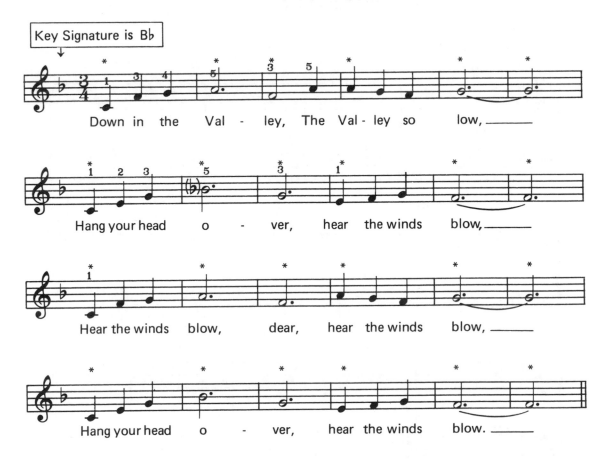

HARMONISING A TUNE

HARMONISING: Where there is an asterisk marked over a bar, using chords F and C add a left hand and pedal accompaniment to 'Down in the Valley'. Listen carefully as you play one or the other chord with the melody to hear which one sounds correct.

NEW SIGNS: A NATURAL ♮ — This sign cancels the use of a previous sharp (♯) or a flat (♭) .

THE SLUR

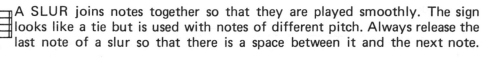

A SLUR joins notes together so that they are played smoothly. The sign looks like a tie but is used with notes of different pitch. Always release the last note of a slur so that there is a space between it and the next note.

Slur sign

Try the following exercise using SLURS.

Exercise 13:

down   up

WE SHALL NOT BE MOVED

Registration: UPPER   Horn or Saxophone   (00 8740 430) Rhythm:
                 LOWER: Flute 8', 4', Diapason   (—— 8853 000)
                 PEDAL: 16' & 8', medium, sustain (5—(3))
                 VIBRATO: ON. Leslie: Fast

Practise the left hand change from chord G to C (bars 8 to 10) first.

58

THE MAJOR KEYS

Much sixteenth to twentieth century Western music is based on a system of organisation called KEYS. These fall into two main categories — MAJOR and MINOR. For the moment we will concentrate on the major pattern. A major key is derived from a set pattern of notes called a MAJOR SCALE. A scale consists of *eight* notes played in alphabetical order to a set pattern of SEMITONES (the shortest distance between any two notes on the keyboard) and TONES (one tone equals two semitones). The pattern is: TONE TONE SEMITONE TONE TONE TONE SEMITONE.

Here it is to form the scale of C MAJOR which starts and ends on the note C.

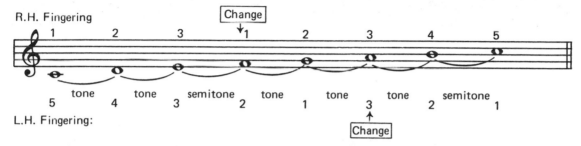

As the scale of C major has no sharps or flats we say that the *key* of C major has no sharps or flats.

However, in order to achieve the correct pattern for the scale of G major, it is necessary to have an F sharp, as the note F natural would provide a semitone between the sixth and seventh notes and a tone between the seventh and eighth notes.

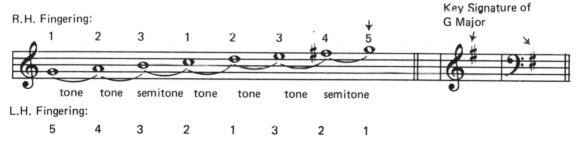

As the scale of G major has an F sharp, we say that the *key signature* of G major is F sharp. The last piece of music you played, 'We Shall Not Be Moved', was in the key of G major. Play the scale of G major and then play this piece of music again.

Here is the scale of F major. The key signature is B flat.

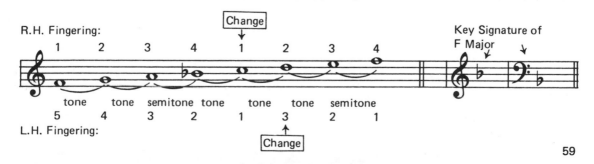

59

Learn the new piece in F major on Page 61. Notice that in the left hand part the notes of each chord are played separately. Practise them as shown below before trying to play them as written in the new version of 'Down In the Valley'.

Exercise 14:

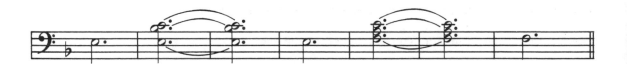

DOWN IN THE VALLEY (second version)

Registration: UPPER: Clarinet, Flute 8', 2⅔' (00 7373 441) Rhythm: Waltz
LOWER: Flute 8' or Bassoon (—— 6554 300)
PEDAL: 8', medium, sustain (4—(3))
VIBRATO: ON. LESLIE/CHORUS ON SLOW

Down in the val - ley, val-ley so low,

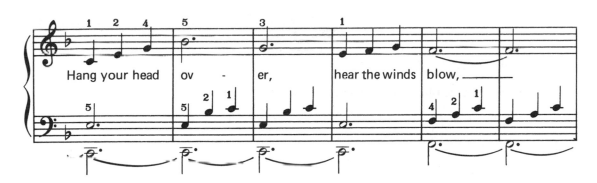

Hang your head ov - er, hear the winds blow,

Hear the winds blow dear, hear the winds blow,

Hang your head ov - er, hear the winds blow.

NEW CHORD: B flat

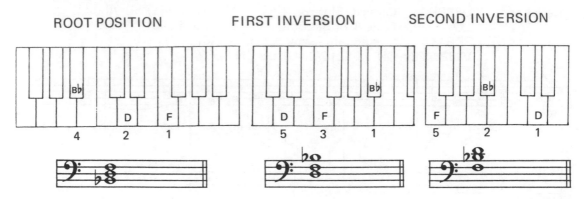

ROOT POSITION   FIRST INVERSION   SECOND INVERSION

CHORD EXTENTIONS — THE SEVENTH CHORD   A chord may be extended by adding new notes to it. If the SEVENTH note above the root of a chord is added, it is called a SEVENTH CHORD. Here is the chord of C with the added seventh — CHORD C7.

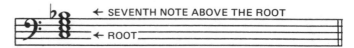

← SEVENTH NOTE ABOVE THE ROOT

← ROOT

This chord can also be played in its various inversions as follows:

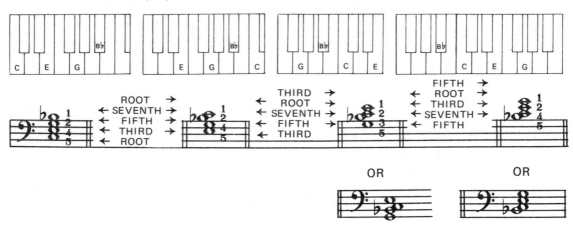

Notice that there are *four* possible positions for a seventh chord.

NEW NOTE: C sharp (♯)

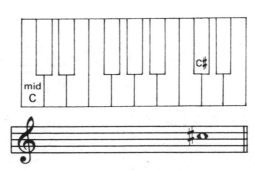

CARELESS LOVE

Registration: UPPER: Trumpet 8', Flute 4', 2⅔', 1' (56 7865 433) Rhythm: Ballad
LOWER: Diapason 8', Flute 8', 4' (—— 5645 000)
PEDAL: 8', medium, sustain (5—(3))
VIBRATO: ON, light. LESLIE/CHORUS: ON, slow

Practise the left hand chord changes very carefully before learning the rest of the piece.

The tie joins the B Flat
An accidental is not cancelled
when tied into another bar.

STACCATO

NEW SIGN: STACCATO  or

A staccato sign is a dot placed *above* and *below* a note. This means that the note must be released as soon as the sound is heard so that it produces a very short sound. Practise some staccato notes in the next exercise. Make sure the 'sustain' button or drawbar is not on before trying this.

Exercise 15:

NEW PEDAL NOTE: B FLAT

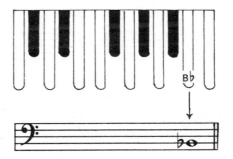

I WAS BORN ABOUT TEN THOUSAND YEARS AGO

Registration: UPPER: String 8', 4', 2'   (34 3576 421) Rhythm: March
                LOWER: Flute 8', 4'   (—— 6500 100)
                PEDAL: 16' + 8', medium, sustain (5—(3))
                VIBRATO: OFF. LESLIE/CHORUS: ON, Fast.

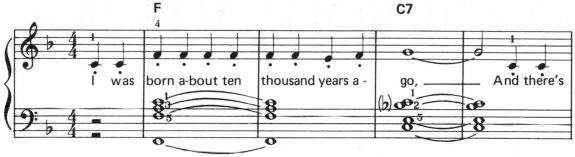

I was born a-bout ten thousand years a - go, ——— And there's

no-thing in the world that I don't know, ——— I saw

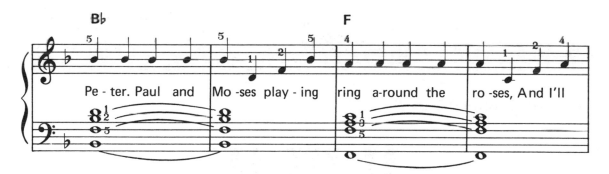

Pe - ter. Paul and Mo - ses play - ing ring a-round the ro -ses, And I'll

lick the guy that says it is -n't so. ———

CHORD G7:

| ROOT POSITION | FIRST INVERSION | SECOND INVERSION | THIRD INVERSION |

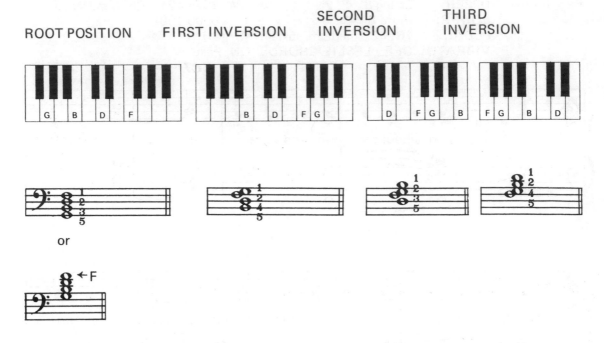

or

Practise the following chord progression before learning the next piece:

Exercise 16:

NEW NOTES: HIGH D, E and F

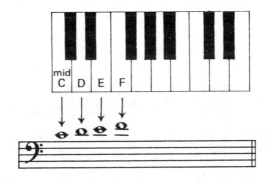

WHEN THE SAINTS

Registration: UPPER: Brass (52 8888 542) Rhythm: Jazz Rock
LOWER: Flutes 8', 4' (—— 8704 000)
PEDAL: 16' + 8', sustain (5—(3))
VIBRATO: ON, heavy. LESLIE/CHORUS: ON, fast.

Notice that the pedal is played on the *first* beat and the left hand part is played on the *third* beat of each bar. Before playing it as written, practise these parts so that they are both played on the *first* beat of each bar.

D MAJOR

TWO NEW CHORDS: D (D7) and A (A7)

(The added seventh is always the note in brackets on the keyboard diagram.)

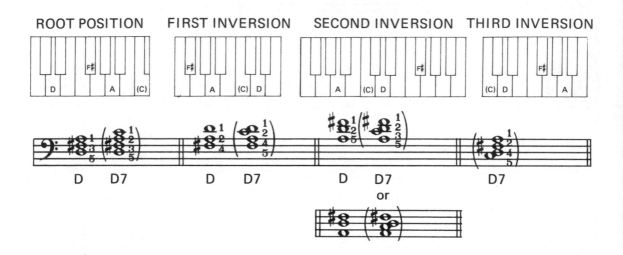

ROOT POSITION   FIRST INVERSION   SECOND INVERSION   THIRD INVERSION

D   D7   D   D7   D   D7   D7

or

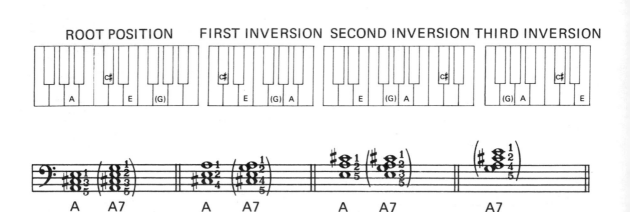

ROOT POSITION   FIRST INVERSION   SECOND INVERSION   THIRD INVERSION

A   A7   A   A7   A   A7   A7

Exercise 17: Chord Changes (D and A)

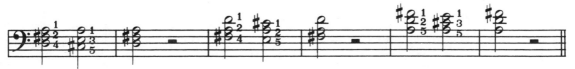

NEW PEDAL NOTES: A and D

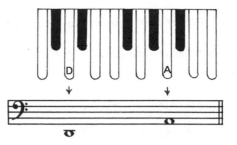

OLD JOE CLARK

Registration:
UPPER: Flute 8', 2⅔', 1' (00 8080 004) Rhythm: March
LOWER: 'Cello 8' (—— 4565 300)
PEDAL: 8', medium, sustain (4—(3))
VIBRATO: OFF. LESLIE/CHORUS: ON, slow.

F sharp and
C sharp

With Vigour

Before trying the 'OOM PAH PAH' bass in the next piece of music, practise the bass so that:

(a) the pedal and left hand parts are played on the first beat of the bar, to the value of a dotted minim e.g.

and (b) then so that the pedal part is played on the *first beat* of each bar, followed by the left hand part on the *second beat,* to the value of a minim. e.g.:

ON TOP OF OLD SMOKEY

Registration: UPPER: Flute 4', Oboe 8'   (00 0822 000) Rhythm: Waltz
                LOWER: Flute 8', Piano   (–– 7304 000)
                PEDAL: 8', medium, sustain (4–(3))

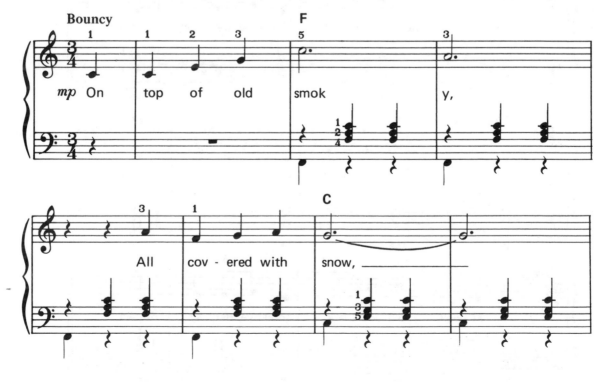

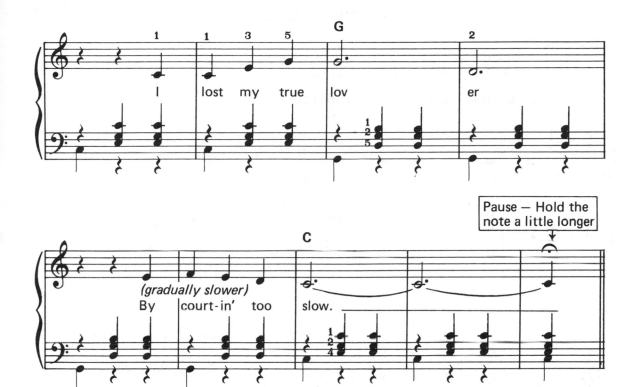

I lost my true lov er

(gradually slower)
By court-in' too slow.

Pause — Hold the note a little longer

FURTHER CHORD EXTENTIONS — THE NINTH CHORD

If the NINTH note above the root is added it is called a ninth chord.

Here is the chord of C with the added ninth — chord C9

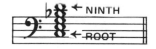

In a ninth chord the root is often omitted.

Here is the chord of G9

Here are the chords of C9 and G9 as they are used in the next piece of music:

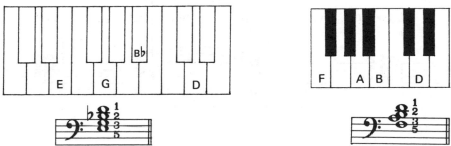

THE RIDDLE SONG

Registration: **UPPER:** Flute 8', Piano (00 8421 000)   Rhythm: Nil
                LOWER: Flute 8'   (—— 6002 000)
                PEDAL: 8', sustain   (4—(2))

Andante (Italian term for 'at a walking pace').

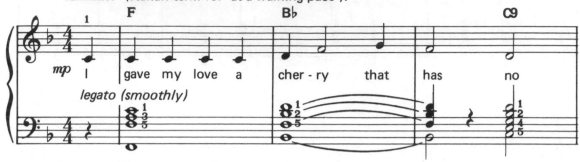

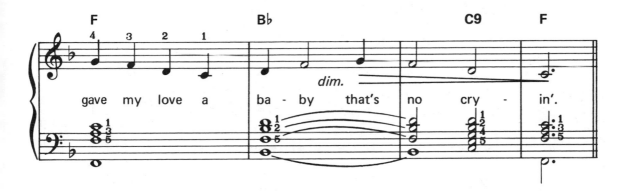

gave my love a ba - by that's no cry - in'.

dim.

THE QUAVER or EIGHTH NOTE: ♪ or 𝅘𝅥𝅮 (written together as 𝅘𝅥𝅮𝅘𝅥𝅮 or 𝅘𝅥𝅮𝅘𝅥𝅮)

A QUAVER equals half the value of a crotchet.

To fit two quavers into one crotchet beat, include the word 'and' between each count e.g.:

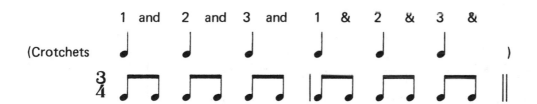

Now try this well known piece of music which contains quavers.

WE WISH YOU A MERRY CHRISTMAS

Registration: UPPER: Percussive (Bells, Piano etc.) (20 6864 332) Rhythm: Waltz
                LOWER: Strings 8', 4'   (—— 7602 000)
                PEDAL: 16' + 8'   (4—(3))
                VIBRATO: ON, light   LESLIE/CHORUS: ON, slow.

Allegro

We wish you a mer-ry Christmas, we wish you a mer-ry Christ-mas we wish you a mer-ry Christ-mas and a hap-py New Year. Good ti-dings we bring, to you and your kin, We wish you a mer-ry Christ-mas and a hap-py New Year.

PEDAL NOTE B

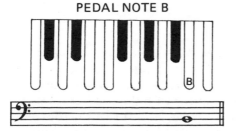

Make sure that you can play the pedal board fluently before trying the rest of the piece.

LI'L LIZA JANE

Registration: UPPER: Piano   (00 6822 000 with percussion) Waltz: Swing
                 LOWER: Flute 8', 4'   (— — 8600 000)
                 PEDAL: 8', sustain   (4—(3))
                 VIBRATO: ON, light. LESLIE/CHORUS: ON, fast.

With bounce

MINOR CHORDS (TRIADS)

So far, although we have not named then as such, all the chords we have learned have been based on MAJOR TRIADS. However, there are different kinds of triads, each with their own particular character of sound. One of these, the MINOR TRIAD, is similar to the construction of a Major Triad. Compare the triad of A major with the triad of A minor written below. Play them both and listen to the sound they make. Notice that the root and fifth of the two chords are the same but the THIRD of the minor triad is a semitone lower than the major one.

Triad of a Major   Triad of a minor

In sheet music, only the letter name is used if a major chord is wanted (e.g. the letter A for A major). For the minor chord, the letter is followed by a small 'm' (e.g. Am for A minor).

Try the next piece of music which includes the A minor chord.

CHORD of A MINOR

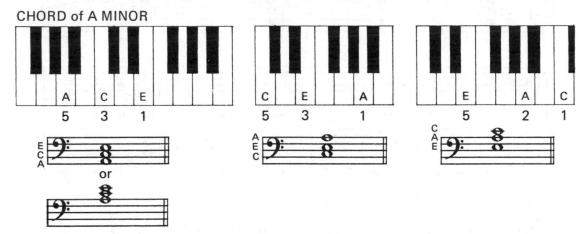

NOTES: LOW G, A and B.

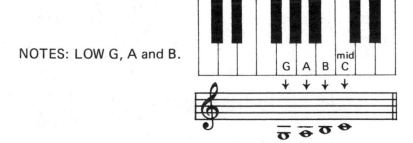

OH! SOLDIER, SOLDIER WON'T YOU MARRY ME? (Traditional)

Registration:
UPPER: Flute 16', 4'. String 8' (63 3723 223) Rhythm: Nil
LOWER: Flute 8', 4'. Reed 8' (‒‒7788 422)
PEDAL: 16'+8' (6‒(3))
VIBRATO: ON, light. LESLIE/CHORUS: ON, fast.

Allegretto (slightly slower than Allegro)

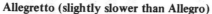

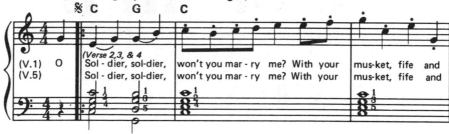

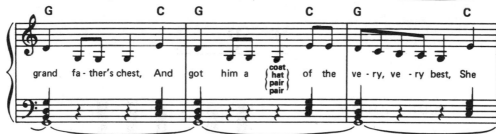

after verse 4 D.S. al Fine 𝄋 → **Go back to this sign and play the music until the word FINE**

77

NEW CHORD: E MINOR

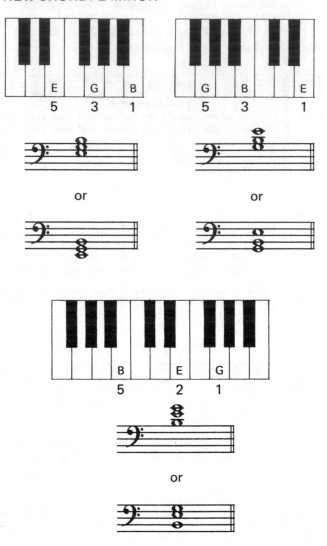

PEDAL NOTE: E

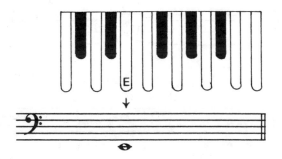

AWAY IN A MANGER

Registration: UPPER: Violin solo (02 3575 332) Rhythm: Nil
LOWER: Flute 8', 4', 2' (–– 6402 000)
PEDAL: 8', medium, sustain (4–(2))
VIBRATO: ON, heavy. LESLIE/CHORUS: On, slow.

Slowly and Smoothly

THE DOTTED CROTCHET or DOTTED HALF NOTE: ♩. or 𝅗𝅥·

A dot placed AFTER a note increases it by half its original value.

♩ +•= 1½ The Dotted Crotchet or Dotted Half Note

Clap the three examples below.

In exercise (b), ties have been introduced to the original rhythm — (exercise a)

In exercise (c), the rhythm should SOUND THE SAME as exercise (b) but the ties have been replaced with dots.

AULD LANG SYNE

Registration: UPPER: Flutes 8', 4', 2'   (00 8808 001)   Rhythm: Slow Waltz
               LOWER: Flute 8'   (— — 8000 000)
               PEDAL   8', sustain   (4—(2))
               VIBRATO: OFF.   LESLIE/CHORUS: ON, slow.

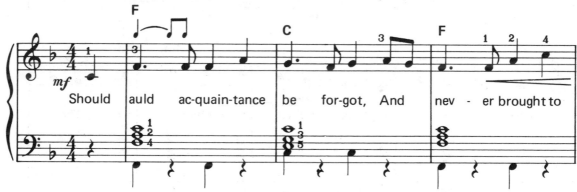

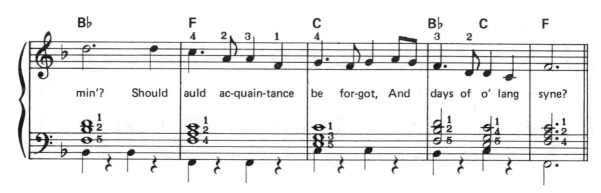

YELLOW ROSE OF TEXAS

Registration: UPPER: Trumpet 8'   (00 6888 543) Rhythm: Slow March
              LOWER: Flute, Woodwind 8', 4' (—— 6864 000)
              PEDAL: 8, sustain   (4—(3))
              VIBRATO: ON, light. LESLIE/CHORUS: ON, fast.

Allegro

There's a yel-low rose in Tex-as, I'm go-ing there to see, No oth-er fel-la knows her, no-bo-dy else but me, She cried so when I left her, it near-ly broke my heart, and if we ev-er meet a-gain, we nev-er more will part.

MICHAEL ROW THE BOAT ASHORE

Registration: UPPER: Flute 16', 4'. String 8' (63 3723 223) Rhythm: Nil
                 LOWER: Flute 8', 4'. Reed 8'   (—— 7788 422)
                 PEDAL: 16' + 8'   (6—(3))
                 VIBRATO: ON, light. LESLIE/CHORUS: ON, fast.

SHARING THE TUNE

So far we have concentrated on right hand melodies with left hand chords. Try the next piece of music which shares the tune between the hands.

LARGO from the 'New World Symphony'

Registration: **UPPER:**   Oboe + Flutes   (00 4763 000)   Rhythm: Nil
                        LOWER: Bassoon or 'Cello solo (–– 4874 000)
                        PEDAL: 8', sustain   (4–(0))
                        VIBRATO: ON, slow, light. **LESLIE/CHORUS:** ON, slow.

83

THE MINOR SCALE

Every major scale shares its key signature with a minor scale. These are called RELATIVE MAJOR and MINOR SCALES. The SIXTH note of a MAJOR scale is the note on which its RELATIVE MINOR scale is constructed, e.g. as the sixth note of the scale of C major is A, its relative minor is A minor.

C MAJOR

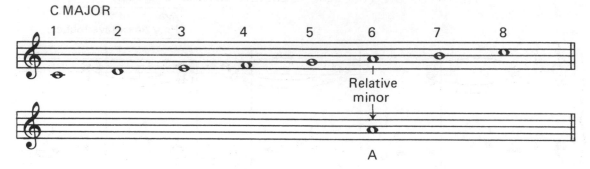

Therefore, the scale of A minor, like its relative major scale C major, has no sharps or flats as its key signature.

There are two kinds of minor scale. In the first, the HARMONIC MINOR, the *seventh* note of the scale is raised by a semitone. This note is NOT included in the key signature but must be raised independently every time it occurs in the music.

THE SCALE OF A HARMONIC MINOR

Play this scale and listen carefully to the effect of the *sixth* to the *seventh* note. The MELODIC MINOR SCALE smooths out the sound of this interval by raising the *sixth* and *seventh notes of the ascending scale* and *lowering them* in the *descending* version.

Play and listen carefully to the scale of 'A' Melodic Minor:

NEW CHORD: E major

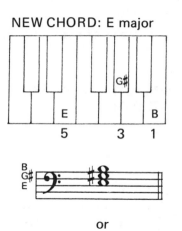

5 3 1

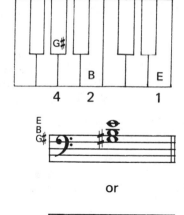

4 2 1

or

or

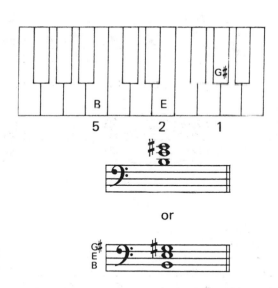

5 2 1

or

Play the following well known song which includes examples of both types of the A minor scale plus the new chord of E major.

GREENSLEEVES

Registration:
UPPER: String 8', 4' (12 3476 421) Rhythm: Nil
LOWER: Flute 8', Piano (– – 8422 000)
PEDAL: 8', sustain (4–(0))
VIBRATO: ON, fast, light. LESLIE/CHORUS: OFF.

A MINOR (Relative major – C):

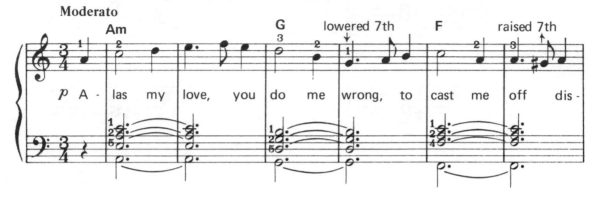

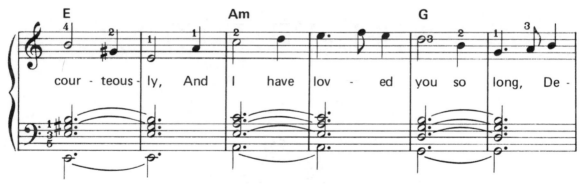

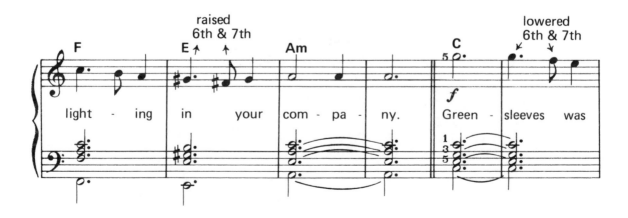

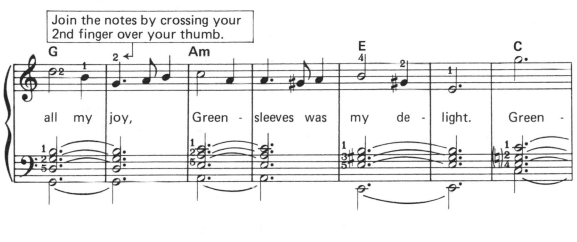

Join the notes by crossing your 2nd finger over your thumb.

all my joy, Green - sleeves was my de - light. Green -

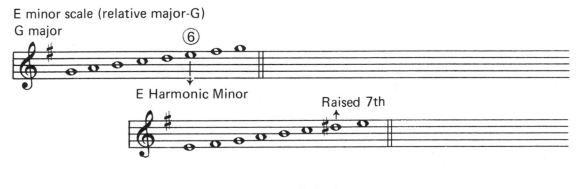

sleeves was my heart of gold, And who but my La - dy Green- sleeves.

E minor scale (relative major-G)
G major

E Harmonic Minor

Raised 7th

E Melodic Minor

Raised 6th & 7th   Lowered 6th & 7th

NEW CHORD: B MAJOR

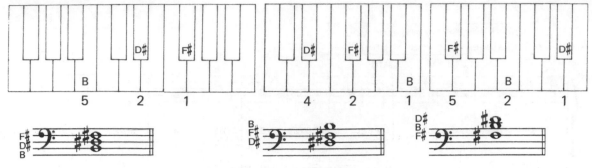

GO DOWN MOSES

Registration: UPPER: 'Cello, Bassoon (67 3576 421)   Rhythm: Nil
                 LOWER: String 8'   (— — 4576 321)
                 PEDAL: 16' + 8' sustain (4—(3))
                 VIBRATO: OFF. LESLIE/CHORUS: ON, slow.

The sign [1.   ] means play this part the first time through, but omit it on the

second playing and go straight to the sign [2.   ]

E MINOR (Relative major — G):

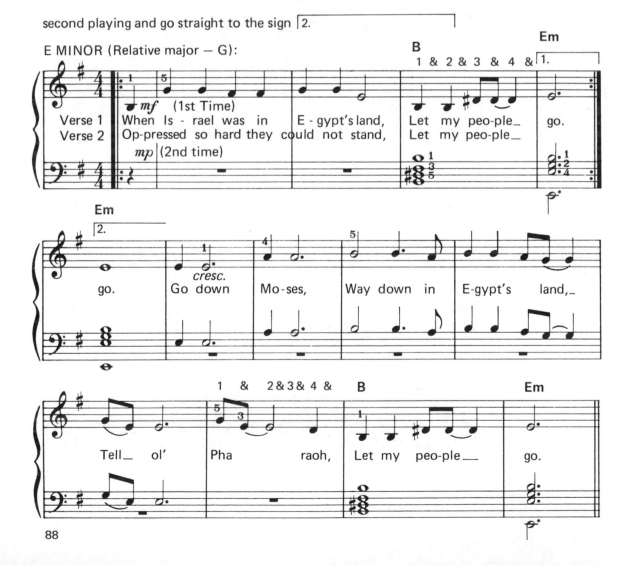

88

D MINOR Scale (Relative major — F)

F Major

⑥

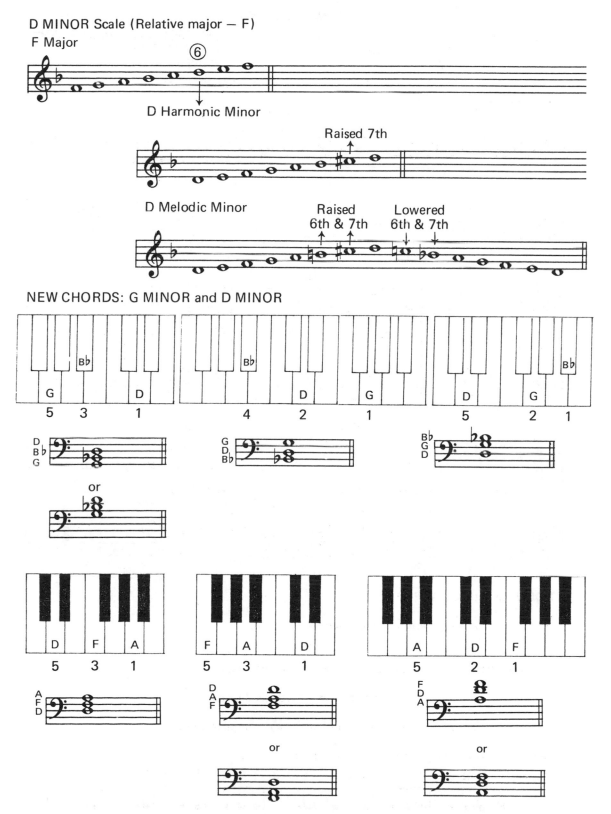

D Harmonic Minor

Raised 7th

D Melodic Minor

Raised 6th & 7th   Lowered 6th & 7th

NEW CHORDS: G MINOR and D MINOR

or

TUM BALALYKA

Registration: **UPPER:** Flutes 8', 4', 2 or harmonica (00 2354 321) **Rhythm: Waltz**
              LOWER: Flutes 8'   (—— 6220 000)
              PEDAL: 8', sustain   (4—(3))
              VIBRATO: ON, light. **LESLIE/CHORUS:** ON, fast.

D MINOR (Relative major — F):

COUNTING IN QUAVERS

$\frac{3}{8}$ = 3 quavers or eighth notes in a bar

In *quaver time*   a quaver   ♪   equals 1 beat

                a crotchet   ♩   equals 2 beats

      and   a dotted crotchet   ♩.   equals 3 beats

Here is a rhythm for you to try in $\frac{3}{8}$ time:

Count: 1 2 3   1 2 3   1 2 3   1 2 3   1 2 3   1 2 3   1 2 3   1 2 3

THE SPANISH GUITAR

Registration: UPPER: Guitar   (00 7372 220)   Rhythm: Waltz
LOWER: Flutes 8', 4' (— — 7400 000)
PEDAL: 8', sustain   (4—(0))
VIBRATO: ON, light.   LESLIE/CHORUS: OFF.

When I was a stu-dent from Ca - diz.____ I played on the

Span-ish Gui - tar, Ching Ching, I used to make love to the

la - dies ____ I think of them still from a - far, Ching, Ching!

Using chords G and D7, add a left hand and pedal accompaniment to 'The Spanish Guitar'.
You could use the following rhythmic idea or one of your own.

$\frac{6}{8}$ time has 6 quavers in a bar divided into 2 dotted crotchet beats:

Try the following rhythm in $\frac{6}{8}$ time. Count 6 quavers in a bar but make sure there is a

slightly louder sound (an accent $>$) on each dotted crotchet beat.

Counting in
Quavers: 1 2 3 4 5 6   1 2 3 4 5 6   1 2 3 4 5 6   1 2 3 4 5 6

Counting in
Dotted crotchets: 1   2   1   2   1   2   1   2

FOR HE'S A JOLLY GOOD FELLOW

𝄐˙	A dotted crotchet rest.	
˙𝄾	A quaver rest.	

Registration: UPPER: Oboe + Flute 8', 4' (00 4675 432) Rhythm: Slow Rock
LOWER: Strings 8' (—— 5674 200)
PEDAL: 8', medium, sustain (4—(3))
VIBRATO: ON, light. LESLIE/CHORUS: ON, fast.

Lively — with Spirit

Go back to the 𝄋 and end at the word *Fine*

A LIFE ON THE OCEAN WAVE

Registration: UPPER: Strings 8', 4'   (34 3576 421)   Rhythm: Nil
              LOWER: Flutes, 8', 4'   (—— 8822 000)
              PEDAL: 16' + 8', sustain (5—(3))
              VIBRATO: ON, light. LESLIE/CHORUS: ON, fast.

With spirit

Go back to the beginning and end at the word *Fine*

D.C. al Fine

PART 3 IDEAS FOR THE FUTURE
FURTHER STEPS

Despite the 'Easy Play' facilities offered by electronic keyboards, this book has concentrated on acquiring the ability to read music. This will help you to choose music via the enormous amount and variety of sheet music from elementary and advanced standards which is available from music shops and libraries.

For further experience, listen and observe as many keyboard players as possible. Again, try not to restrict yourself to any particular style of music.

There are also many organ clubs where members are given the opportunity to discuss and hear the latest available instruments and large manufacturers hold regular demonstrations and exhibitions of their instruments. Playing with other musicians is an excellent way of improving your musicianship and repertoire. Your school, music shop, local or music paper should help you to find others with similar interests.

If you are not already having lessons, finding a teacher would probably accelerate your progress.

HINTS ON REGISTRATION

Whether your instrument has Drawbars, Presets, Combinations, Solo or Accompaniment voices, the objective is still the same — to create a satisfying balance between the parts of the type of piece being played.

Drawbars can produce a wide range of tone from different pitch combinations. It is best to start with combinations of mellow flute sounds: 16' 8' 4' 2' 1', and then find new sounds by adding mixture drawbars such as: $5^{1}/_{3}$, $2^{2}/_{3}$, or $1^{3}/_{5}$, to give more colour.
If there is not enough 'bite' to the note, add a percussive drawbar to your selection. Avoid using too much sustain or reverberation as these can easily make the sound heavy and blurred.

Presets on keyboards now give sounds that can be used independently for a fine solo or accompaniment. Your ear is still the best judge of a suitable combination of presets, so listen to as much music as you can and then experiment with new registrations. For example, you might be using Brass Ensemble and Solo Piano for the right hand, with Orchestral Strings and soft Flutes accompanying.

The experienced player will have a feeling for the way one particular instrument blends with another, without making the sound too complicated.

Remember that many portable keyboards select only one preset at a time and only the more versatile keyboards and larger organs offer the layering of sounds together. Try to build up a sound combination that makes the music interesting because of its changing timbre. For example, you might have a Harpsichord attack, while the Piano gradually decays, to leave a soft Flute with Sustain.

The success of a performance often comes from a subtle or dramatic use of registration. Explore all the sound combinations that your keyboard offers, so that every piece you play holds the listener's attention. Having found an interesting preset or combination for a piece, try using it with some effects or sound processing devices such as vibrato, chorus or arpeggio. The right choice of voices and the right balance between them is as important as playing the right notes.

SPECIAL EFFECTS

There are THREE types of special effects on an electronic keyboard. The *first type* covers the tabs or preset switches that select special sound effects for copying traditional instruments like Banjo, or the most unusual synthetic sounds. Here are some examples:

BANJO/MANDOLIN — A strumming effect is produced simply be pressing a key (with a repeat rate often variable).

HAWAIIAN GUITAR — A typical glide up to the note is heard on each new key play, ('new key play' means that all notes in use on the manual are released beforehand).

WAH-WAH — A synthesised filter effect that sounds like the modern 'Wah' pedal used by guitarists.

FUZZ/OVERDRIVE — The sound signal is distorted by overloading an amplification stage for a popular guitar effect. It is best on single notes.

NOISE — A white or pink noise that can make natural sounds like the sea and wind, or percussive and special effects, like a 'spaceship take-off'.

The *second type* covers many different controls that add extra 'performance control'. Many of these require a different technique of playing and often operate from a special mechanism, electronic contacts or pads beneath the keyboard: e.g.

TOUCH SENSITIVITY — Which gives you the kind of volume control it is possible to achieve by depressing the keys of an accoustic piano.

DYNAMIC TOUCH CONTROL — Once a key is depressed, further pressure on it will (PRESSURE CONTROL) bring in a number of effects, e.g. changes of pitch, vibrato or tone.

INITIAL/AFTER TOUCH — A combination of the above effects. Voices like Harmonica can be made to change breath attack (initial) and add vibrato (after). Sometimes pressure control (after touch) will allow other instruments to be added to existing sounds, such as piano with strings.

DOUBLE TOUCH — Pressing a tab of this kind harder will mechanically release other tabs selected.

MODULATION — The most frequently used modulation effects are VIBRATO and TREMOLO. Vibrato is a smooth cyclic change of pitch often used on traditional string and wind instruments. Tremolo is a cyclic variation of volume, as heard on low flute notes. Modulation effects often have a DELAY before operating to be more realistic.

SLALOM — A polyphonic slide of pitch up to the played chord.

PORTAMENTO — A smooth pitch slide from one note to the next (monophonic or polyphonic) with variable slide time.

GLISSANDO — Sounds all the black and white notes between two notes played on the keyboard, with variable slide time, (monophonic or polyphonic).

KNEE LEVER — Some larger console and portable self-standing instruments have this for right knee operation, controlling pitch, tone or sustain.

95

PEDAL SWITCH	— A built-in volume pedal may also have left and right switches that operate as you rock your right foot. It can be used for starting a rhythm or arpeggio, giving auto-wah, slide or sustain.
TRANSPOSE	— A rotary click-feel switch, set of buttons, or dialled-up display control to transpose the overall pitch of the instrument to a new key.
TEMPO-TOUCH	— The touch buttons allow the tempo of the rhythm unit, 'Easy Play' accompaniment and arpeggio to be altered.

The *third type of special effect* covers sound processing controls that can improve the final sound of the voices, REVERBERATION, for example, is essential to give an instrument's sound a gradual volume decay as in a concert hall. Without it, (or some other ECHO effect), a keyboard will sound very 'dry'.

The following considerably enrich the sound turning solo violins into string orchestras by means of an electronic phasing effect. Some spread the sound into a broad stereo image, like a large orchestra in front of you:

ORCHESTRA, ENSEMBLE, SYMPHONIC CHORUS, SYMPHONIC STEREO, MULTI-CHORUS, CHORUS, CASCADING STRINGS, AUDIO EXPANDER, STEREOPHAZE SOUND, SOUND-A-RAMA.

SUSTAIN	— An important control that simply extends the time it takes for sound to die away. On portable keyboards it can be a good substitute for reverberation.
DETUNE	— Every key plays two notes that are slightly out of tune with one another to give richer sounds, or more extreme 'honky-tonk' piano, accordion, or celeste effects.
DIGITAL FLUTE ANIMATION	— Another enhancing feature that gives the sound movement and depth.
COUPLERS AND PRESETS	— On large instruments with more than one manual, it is often necessary and desirable to couple together one or more sections. Sometimes a complete section can be selected from one tab or button, while sophisticated instruments allow the player to programme his own choice of voices for recall from a button later. CANCEL tabs turn off couplers and MEMORY tabs hold on a selected sound indefinitely.

Some instruments, particularly organ types, also contain controls for Leslie Tone Cabinet simulation, either mechanical or electronic — the latter becoming increasingly popular. The special rotating sound creates two main effects. A slow rotation (called CHORALE or CELESTE) a church-like depth is introduced, while fast rotation (called TREMOLO, TREMULANT or THEATRICAL) in combination with plenty of percussion footages gives the typical theatre organ, or jazz organ sound.

ACCESSORIES

There are a large range of optional accessories that can be used with keyboards and these are usually listed in the manufacturer's catalogue;

For example:

carrying cases; covers; floor stands; power supplies for portables that can be battery rechargeable, mains power pack or car battery types.

Drum machines are available for use with all types of instruments and often have superior percussion sounds to built-in designs. Free-standing pedal boards can be added to a single or dual manual keyboard and a good music stool can improve your comfort when playing. Separate reverberation or echo units will give greater depth to your sound. If your keyboard has several outputs, a volume pedal accessory can control each one independently, and portables often have sockets for headphones, external microphones or sustain footswitch.

Most manufacturers also sell keyboard combo amplifiers suitable for lounge, small halls or larger auditoriums.

Recording music is part of the enjoyment of being a musician and you can purchase a low cost portable multitrack recorder (or Portastudio) that will allow you to create your own electro-music studio around your keyboard.

IMPROVISATION

Improvising or making up your own music as you go along is the first step to producing some of your own compositions. Try out some simple chord progressions e.g.

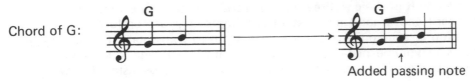

When you are satisfied with the sound of certain chord progressions, using notes from each chord as it is played, add a melody part. You can extend the range of your melody by either bridging the gap between two notes of a chord with a PASSING NOTE (p.n.) e.g.

Chord of G:

Added passing note

or, adding a note which is directly above or below a repeated note — AUXILIARY NOTE (a.n.) e.g.

Added auxiliary note

MORE ABOUT CHORDS

So far we have only learned major and minor triads, added sevenths and added ninths. It is possible to add any note to a chord using the number above the root method e.g.

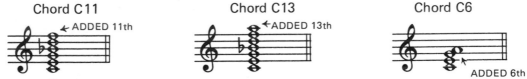

Chord C11 — ADDED 11th

Chord C13 — ADDED 13th

Chord C6 — ADDED 6th

Try some of your own.

These chords may also be slightly altered by raising or lowering any of their notes e.g.

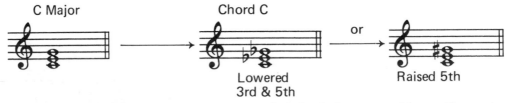

C Major

Chord C — Lowered 3rd & 5th

or

Raised 5th

The next section includes most of the major triads in their root positions. Remember that these may be converted into minor triads by lowering the middle note by a semitone or may be extended to form added note chords.

For any further information on the reading of music and additional signs and symbols we recommend another book in this series —

'How to Read Music' by Roger Evans.

CHORD DIRECTORY

NB: Although if your keyboard has pedals you will probably not use chords in root position, this section is given as an aid to finding the notes of basic major triads.

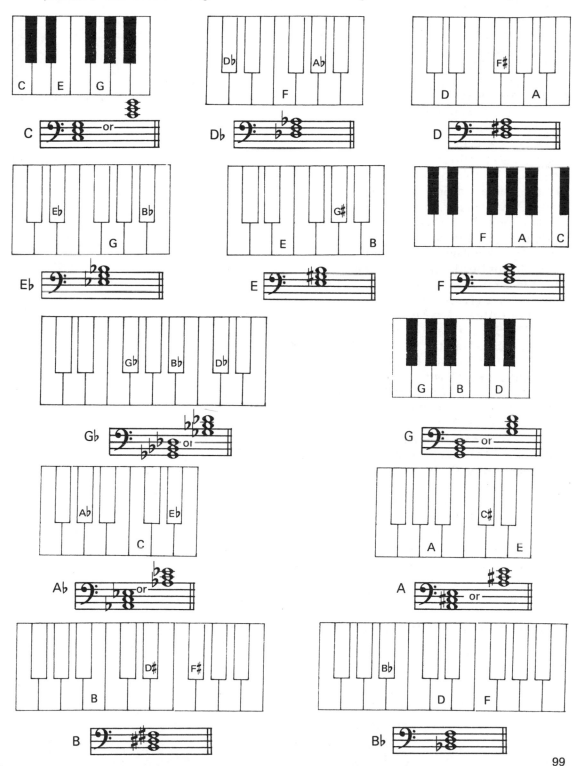

MUSIC IN THIS BOOK

(All musical arrangements and exercises by Rosalyn Asher)

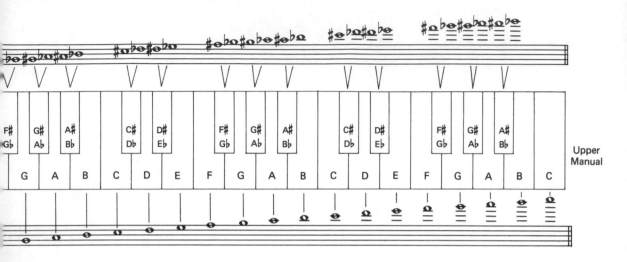

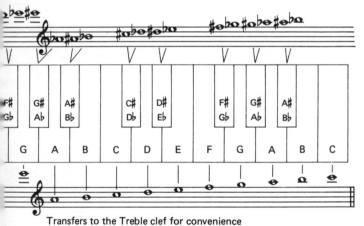

Upper Manual

Lower Manual
(Could lie directly under
Upper Manual

Transfers to the Treble clef for convenience

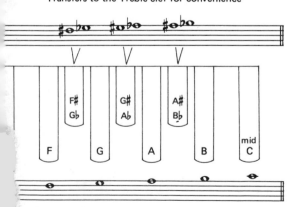

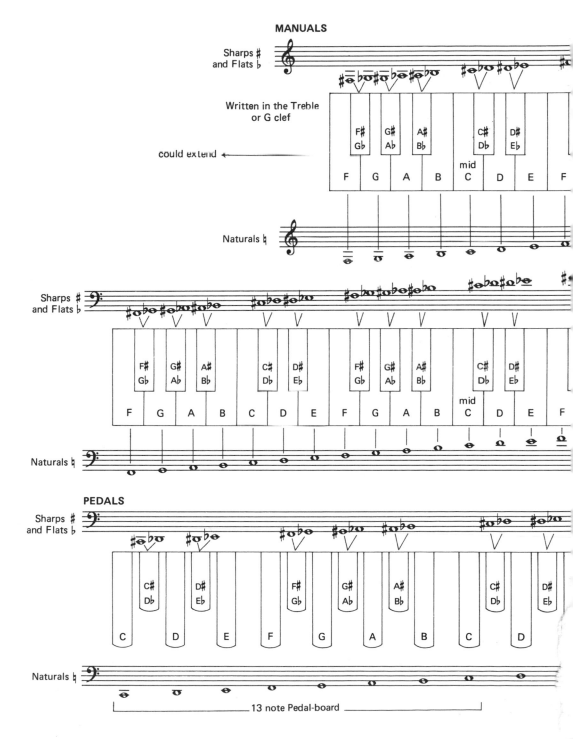